PRAISE FOR *THOUGHTS ARE THINGS*

"Bob and Greg make a great team—Napoleon Hill's legacy lives on!"

—BRIAN TRACY, international best-selling author

"An excellent observation on how people create their own reality."

—DAVE LINIGER, cofounder of RE/MAX

"This book has the ability to impact many lives around the globe."

—DR. DENIS WAITLEY, author, keynote lecturer, and productivity consultant

"When you're ready to change everything about your life, you have to change your thoughts, which control your actions and your results. This book is where you begin."

—JIM STOVALL, best-selling author of *The Ultimate Gift*

"What a great book. I recommend it highly."

—FRANK SHANKWITZ, cofounder, Make-A-Wish Foundation

"This book is a fantastic example of applying Napoleon Hill's classic teachings."

—LES BROWN, author of *The Motivator*

T0200752

THOUGHTS
ARE THINGS

✦

THOUGHTS
ARE THINGS

Turning Your Ideas into Realities

THE THINK AND GROW RICH® SERIES

BOB PROCTOR and GREG S. REID

JEREMY P. TARCHER/PENGUIN
an imprint of Penguin Random House
New York

JEREMY P. TARCHER/PENGUIN
An imprint of Penguin Random House LLC
375 Hudson Street
New York, New York 10014

First trade paperback edition 2015

Most Tarcher/Penguin books are available
at special quantity discounts for bulk purchase for
sales promotions, premiums, fund-raising, and educational needs.
Special books or book excerpts also can be created to fit specific needs.
For details, write: SpecialMarkets@penguinrandomhouse.com.

The Library of Congress has catalogued the hardcover edition as follows:

Proctor, Bob.
Thoughts are things : turning your ideas into realities / Bob Proctor, Greg S. Reid.
p.   cm.
ISBN 978-0-399-16917-5
1. New Thought.   2. Creative ability.   I. Reid, Greg S.   II. Title.
BF639.P867   2014   2014038464
158.1—dc23
ISBN 978-0-399-17497-1 (paperback)

Printed in the United States of America

BOOK DESIGN BY TANYA MAIBORODA

CONTENTS

✦

FOREWORD

⤜⤛⊷

"THOUGHTS ARE THINGS" ARE THE FIRST THREE WORDS
in the quintessential work on success, *Think and
Grow Rich*, and represent the starting point of all
achievement. Have you ever had a good idea? Of
course you have! But have you ever made money
from one of your good ideas?

The most successful businesses are created by
solving a problem or serving a need. The initial
thought triggers your entrepreneurial spirit, and
instantly creates intellectual property that be-
longs to you. As defined by the World Intellectual
Property Organization, "*Intellectual property* refers
to creations of the mind, such as inventions; literary and artistic works; designs; and symbols,
names and images used in commerce." It is the intangible asset that results from human intellect,

creativity, innovation, and know-how and from reputation and goodwill created by relationships with others.

Only a few decades ago, the value of the bulk of US corporate assets was from tangible assets, such as property, plant, and equipment. Intangibles, such as intellectual property, represented only approximately 20 percent of the value of corporate assets. However, by 2005, that ratio of intangible to tangible corporate assets had essentially reversed; the market value of the S&P 500 was approximately 80 percent intangible assets. According to the US Department of Commerce, "[t]he entire U.S. economy relies on some form of intellectual property, because virtually every industry either produces or uses it."

In other words, the future of our economy depends on intellectual property triggered by entrepreneurial thoughts! No longer do you need vast amounts of capital to start and build a business. With this shift in the importance of intellectual property, combined with the ease of communication provided by the Internet, it has never been easier to build a business around your good ideas.

My business success has come from creating intellectual property related to educational products like books and games and then building the businesses to deliver them. I had the pleasure of working closely with my wonderful husband, Michael Lechter, who is recognized internationally for his intellectual property expertise.

Once you think of a way to solve a problem or serve a need, you may also want to put certain legal protection mechanisms in place (things like patents, trademark and copyright registrations, and contractual agreements) and you will want to create the system that will allow you to deliver the solution or provide the service. That system creates your business . . . a business born from your thoughts.

This book has been written for you at the perfect time. It shares the stories of some incredible people who not only built successful businesses using this model, but made significant positive impacts on their communities in the process. As you read their stories, keep a journal nearby so you can record the thoughts that spring into your mind!

Your next thought could ignite your entrepreneurial spirit, creating intellectual property for you . . . and the beginnings of your next business. Here's to your million-dollar idea!

—SHARON LECHTER, CPA, CGMA
Author of *Think and Grow Rich for Women*
and *Save Wisely, Spend Happily*
Coauthor of *Outwitting the Devil,*
Three Feet from Gold, and *Rich Dad Poor Dad*

INTRODUCTION

*You are the master of your destiny. You can influence,
direct, and control your own environment. You can
make your life what you want it to be.*

—NAPOLEON HILL

EVERY YEAR HAS ITS HIGH POINTS: ACHIEVEMENTS AND
advancements that leave an indelible mark upon
history and upon society as a whole.

The year 1937 was no exception. In fact, I consider it one of the most significant years in all of
human experience.

This was the year that saw the release of
Walt Disney's first full-length animated feature
film . . . the emergence of a thrilling and contro-
versial new artist named Pablo Picasso . . . and
the completion of the Golden Gate Bridge. Nylon
was patented in 1937, and Howard Hughes made
his record-breaking coast-to-coast voyage. It was

also the year *The Hobbit* had its literary debut, as well as *Of Mice and Men* and *Out of Africa*.

Remarkable as they are, however, it's not any of these milestones that makes 1937 such a significant historical moment, in my estimation. It was the publication of another groundbreaking book, a book that would go on to profoundly influence tens of millions of lives, right up through this very day, and undoubtedly beyond it.

The story behind the creation of this miraculous work is one of the more fascinating tales of the early twentieth century—one that perfectly captures the near-mythological dynamism, excitement, and can-do spirit of the era.

❊

It all started in the mind of the great steel magnate and philanthropist Andrew Carnegie. Carnegie's was the ultimate rags-to-riches tale. Born penniless in Scotland, he emigrated to America with his parents as a boy, and eventually rose to become the wealthiest businessman of his time, founding the company that would eventually form one of the cornerstones of US Steel.

Carnegie knew what he'd done to achieve his enormous wealth and success, and he had a theory. He was convinced that great achievement was a matter of doing a few certain things in a certain way. He believed that these certain things were the common denominator shared by all successful people. And he was convinced that if they could be discerned and delineated in a step-by-step formula, anyone, of any background or circumstance, could become wealthy and successful as well, simply by following it.

So he enlisted the help of a young reporter to help him prove his theory—and perhaps change the world in the process.

In 1908, this reporter, Napoleon Hill, had been assigned to interview the great industrialist as part of his publication's series on successful men. Originally slated to take three hours, the interview went on for three full days and three full nights before it was complete.

Even more remarkable than the longevity of the interview was the offer Carnegie made to his visitor when the interview wound to a close:

> Young man, if you are willing to work for me—for free—for twenty years, I will send you on a mission to meet the most powerful and influential leaders of our time. During these encounters, you will discover and create the first-ever formula for personal success.

It was a stunning proposition, one not many people would have had the guts or foresight to accept. But Napoleon Hill wasn't just anyone. He was somehow able to comprehend, in just a few seconds, the incredible potential in the opportunity before him—for both himself and the world. He looked the great man squarely in the eye and said, "Mr. Carnegie, not only will I accept your proposal, I promise I will complete it."

Hill didn't know it at the time, but he wasn't the first recipient of Carnegie's remarkable proposition. More than 250 men had been presented with the great man's unconventional offer.

He was, however, the first one to accept it.

He also didn't realize until later just how crucial his decisiveness on the matter had been. A stickler for action, Carnegie had privately decided he would give his guest just sixty seconds to make up his mind once the proposition had been laid on the table. He knew what the job would entail, and he wasn't interested in wafflers. When Hill walked out of the office, his host pulled from his pocket the stopwatch he had started. There were still thirty-one seconds left.

Clearly, Carnegie had found his man.

Carnegie had promised to furnish Hill a letter of recommendation to the titans of the age, assuring him that when these men saw who had sent him, they would give him all the time he needed. True to his word, he gave the young author access to the brains of the era's great thought leaders, including Thomas Edison, Henry Ford, Alexander Graham Bell, and the Rockefellers, among others.

Hill interviewed them all—and hundreds more—over a period of many years, shaping along the way the formula Carnegie had envisioned. In 1937, nearly twenty years after setting out on his quest, he published his findings in what would go on to become one of the best-selling and most influential books of all time—*Think and Grow Rich*.

In this slim volume, Hill presented the distillation of all he had learned in what he termed the Philosophy of Achievement. This philosophy consisted of thirteen individual principles, or "keys to success," which included:

1. Definiteness of Purpose
2. The Power of the Master Mind
3. Going the Extra Mile
4. Applied Faith
5. A Pleasing Personality
6. Self-discipline
7. Positive Mental Attitude
8. Enthusiasm
9. Personal Initiative
10. Learning from Adversity and Defeat

Hill theorized that these keys would unlock the door to lifelong success, abundance, and fulfillment for anyone who mastered them. It was a tantalizing promise, of course, but it soon became clear that there was real substance behind it. People who faithfully applied the principles discovered that, lo and behold, they *worked*—in exactly the way Hill said they would. Indeed, this was a formula for success: solid, reliable, and available to anyone and everyone who wanted it.

Carnegie's theory was proven . . . and a legend was born.

It is almost impossible to overstate the impact that *Think and Grow Rich* has had since its publication. At the time of Hill's death in 1970, it had already sold twenty million copies. Today, that number is estimated at close to seventy million— and those numbers don't take into account the unknown millions who received the book from someone else, or picked it up at a used-book store or the library. It is one of the cornerstones of the modern self-growth movement and has been openly credited as the inspiration behind many of the most successful corporations, organizations, and careers in the world.

My own first encounter with this life-changing book occurred in 1961, more than half a century after Hill's momentous first meeting with Andrew Carnegie. Seeing the state my young life was in, an older and much wiser friend (whom I soon came to see as a kind of guardian angel) handed me a copy of *Think and Grow Rich* and rather strongly suggested I read it.

My life was never the same again.

Up until that point I was, in a word, lost. I had a job that was going nowhere. I was in an amount of debt I couldn't imagine being able to repay. I had no plans, no ambition of any kind . . . no vision of a future meaningfully different or better than the present situation I was in.

Think and Grow Rich changed all of that. Instantly.

Through *Think and Grow Rich*, my eyes were

opened to a universe of possibilities of whose existence I previously had absolutely no awareness. And the wondrous "aha" at the heart of it all was the sudden understanding of the limitless potential that lay within my own mind—more specifically, the enormous, extraordinary power of my *thoughts*.

Now, this wasn't something I'd ever considered before. To the extent that I'd given any consideration at all to the "why" behind my circumstances, I saw myself the way many people in the world do: as a victim. I had no idea that I'd thought myself into the mess I was in. It certainly never occurred to me that I could think my way out of it.

This realization ignited a fierce, profound passion in me. I became ravenous for, sought out, and found as much information and insight on the subject of self-development as I possibly could. I found it in other books, such as James Allen's immortal *As a Man Thinketh* and Wallace Wattles's masterpiece *The Science of Getting Rich*. I found it in mentors like the legendary "dean of personal development" Earl Nightingale and his business partner, Lloyd Conant, whom I eventually worked with at their pioneering company, Nightingale-Conant.

And over and over again, at every chance I got, I reread the book that started it all for me: Napoleon Hill's *Think and Grow Rich*.

The more I filled my mind with these ideas, the richer my life became. Materially, to be sure. Within a year of reading *Think and Grow Rich*, my annual income went from $4,000 a year to $175,000. Within three years, it increased to over $1 million. I have bought and sold companies in countries around the world, written best-selling books, appeared in films and on television programs, consulted for the world's top organizations, advised leaders of nations, and reaped great financial rewards from my endeavors.

But since that day so many years ago, I have "grown rich" in so many other ways besides: rich in awareness and understanding; rich in friendship and love; rich in freedom—the amazing freedom that comes from realizing that I, not anyone or anything else, have the power to determine my own destiny. Most rewarding of all, I've grown rich in the incredibly fulfilling knowledge that I have played a part in helping many others to find that wonderful freedom and realize their dreams as well.

The fire that *Think and Grow Rich* first lit within me all those years ago has never diminished, and it burns to this day. Through the Proctor Gallagher Institute, my partner and cofounder, Sandy Gallagher, and I, along with our dedicated team, strive each day in countless ways to, in the words of our vision statement, "improve the quality of lives globally by elevating the quality of thoughts individually." Lying at the very heart of this vision, inspiring and guiding it, is, of course, Napoleon Hill's fundamental message of self-directed, mind-powered success.

All of which is to say that *thoughts matter.* They matter enormously. One single, powerful thought can create a ripple effect that touches and transforms more lives, in more ways than you could possibly fathom.

Napoleon Hill lived in an era of exceptional thought leaders—individuals whose names fill us with awe and respect even now, and whose accomplishments continue to influence our lives on a daily basis.

Yet our own era is also replete with such visionaries and achievers. They are the beneficiaries, directly or indirectly, of Hill's philosophy—men and women who came of age in a world and culture already suffused with the idea that, within one's own magnificent mind, lies the potential to be, do, and have *anything* one can imagine or desire.

In the chapters that follow, we're going to meet some of these leaders. We're going to examine their achievements, the thoughts that lie behind them, and the different ways that those thoughts are reverberating out in the world, impacting and transforming lives far beyond their own, shaping our future just as the leaders of Hill's day shaped theirs.

As you discover these leaders, hear their stories, and draw inspiration from their accomplishments, remember this: *What they've done, you can do, too.* You don't have to look outside of yourself to find the power to do so. You already possess it. It is the power of thought . . . the power of your *mind*. To unleash it, you simply need to believe and act.

So . . . begin. Begin now. In the words of my great inspiration and mentor, Napoleon Hill, "Do not wait. The time will never be 'just right.'"

CHAPTER 1

THE LUCK LIE

*Successful men become successful only because they acquire
the habit of thinking in terms of success.*
—NAPOLEON HILL

THE WORLD IS FILLED WITH INDIVIDUALS WHO SEEM TO
magically attract success. Opportunity seems to
appear out of the blue and find them, without
requiring them to look for it. They are the Carn-
egies and Fords of yesterday and the Trumps and
Gateses of today.

Some people credit this kind of success to
luck. But the truth is, every individual who has
created success on a repeated basis has followed
a pattern of doing the right things in the right
order. Success leaves traces, and when we study
these "serial achievers," we can backtrack and

identify the patterns they have habitually applied toward each.

Napoleon Hill once broached this very subject with Andrew Carnegie when he asked him, "Is it not true that success is often the result of luck?" Carnegie's thoughts on the matter were characteristically direct: "If you analyze my definition of success, you will see that there is no element of luck about it. A man may, and sometimes men do, fall into opportunities through mere chance, or luck; but they have a way of falling out of these opportunities the first time opposition overtakes them."

In other words, opportunities may present themselves randomly and without apparent reason, but success cannot be attained only by seizing an opportunity. One must follow certain principles in a habitual way in order to create success from those opportunities.

Carnegie was, of course, his own case in point. The industrialist, steel magnate, investor, salesperson, and scholar knew that his extraordinary successes were not due to luck but rather to his consistent application of the same set of proven success principles to each new opportunity that arose.

Trey Urbahn also acknowledges that being in the right place when opportunity presents itself is an advantage. But, like Carnegie, it's not this particular brand of "luck" he credits with his success. It's the ability to identify that opportunity, act on it, and apply certain principles in order to maximize it.

Trey has been behind the scenes of some incredible companies, including JetBlue Airways, OneSky, and Azul Linhas Aéreas Brasileiras. Among his most noteworthy accomplishments, however, was the founding of the discount travel website Priceline.com.

Backtrack through Trey's successes, and a pattern becomes readily apparent.

FINDING OPPORTUNITIES BY
DOING WHAT YOU LOVE

❖

When asked about the defining factor in pursuing any professional endeavor, Trey says that money was never a consideration for him.

"I've never chased the money. I chased opportunities. I've always done what I liked, and there were times I discovered I wasn't doing what I liked, and I made life changes when that happened."

Trey's background in the airline industry didn't limit the opportunities he explored and seized. Being involved in the founding of Priceline provided him with a unique opportunity to stretch past his comfort zone and expand his horizons. While it still had its teeth in the familiar world of the airline industry, its uniqueness and strength came from the fact that it was Internet based—a relatively novel concept at the time.

"It was the ground zero of the Internet bubble. Jay Walker had an idea to turn commerce on its side. At the time, I had a consulting firm and had the opportunity to work with Jay. My background was in the airline business, so we basically built Priceline as buyer-driven commerce, going to airlines to see how we could get good prices. It was a time when people were looking at the Internet and saying, 'This is going to change the world.'"

Their venture proved to do just that.

"We went from an idea, which was selling airline tickets, to its peak, where we sold thirty thousand airline tickets a day. We were impacting significantly the load factors of the airlines who were our primary customers. Some didn't participate initially—we started with two airlines, and after moving a ton of business their way, others participated."

While Priceline initially focused on the airline business, an industry in which Trey was able to contribute his expertise, experience, and relationships, it eventually expanded into hotels, which still kept its main focus on the travel industry but enabled him to gain knowledge and expertise in new areas—and, true to Trey's pattern, find and act on new opportunities in those areas.

As so often happens when a new idea is presented to the world, people initially thought Trey and his team were crazy. But he was able to recognize the opportunity and the fact that the time was right. They had a vision, they delivered that vision with articulation and excitement, and their enthusiasm and belief proved contagious. Soon, people wanted to follow their energy.

"There are cases in life and smart people who were never able to find the right opportunity. I think part of it is if you do what you do and you like it, that's more likely to happen than if you lose the spark of what makes you go to work every day."

Toiling away in a job you hate isn't likely to drop any spectacular opportunities on your doorstep, mainly because you're too preoccupied with your dissatisfaction to be able to see them. But when, like Trey, you have a genuine interest in your business and a passion for what you do, the opportunities you need will show up for you—in a way that may seem like "luck" but is, in fact, the natural order of the universe.

Work Your Strengths, Hire Your Weaknesses

⟫—⟪

What makes one idea or thought more successful than another: the idea itself, the execution thereof, or a combination of both? Trey's experience suggests it's something else altogether.

I would say that I've had a lot of ideas in my life, some of which I've executed well and others that I haven't executed well. What I have learned is that the best idea is one that grows with the participation of other people, because you start with an idea, and the ability to execute an idea on your own is always going to be limited. So surround yourself with people that you trust to sort out the ninety percent that is a really good idea and take the ten percent that needs some work and move it in a different direction. You need people to help you sort out whatever percentage it is that is good or bad.

In other words, don't fall so deeply in love with your original idea that you become inflexible. Be open to improvements and suggestions. Countless potentially great ideas have been so cradled and protected by their generators for fear they would change beyond recognition that they never saw the light of day. Consider the possibility that your idea may have both strengths and weaknesses. Then muster the courage to surround yourself with people who tell you what you need to hear, and not what you want to hear.

Trey knows his weaknesses, so he makes a point of surrounding himself with people who complement him and balance them out. As a result, he becomes stronger.

Always hire people who are better than you. It's sometimes hard to do, but it's always a worthwhile goal. I've worked for big and little companies, and you will find people who define themselves by themselves because they are afraid to hire people who will outshine them. Those people very rarely end up shining. It's the people who can channel the genius of others around them who end up making things happen.

He refers to this strategy as "working his strengths and hiring his weaknesses." And it's one of the secrets to his multiple successes.

Napoleon Hill defined a genius as "one who has taken full possession of his own mind and directed it toward objectives of his own choosing, without permitting outside influences to discourage or mislead him." By knowing his goal and seeking participants who can help him to improve his idea or plan, Trey has created a success model based on mutual benefit that he can replicate over and over again.

There are plenty of people out there who are ready, willing, and able to assist you in implementing your thoughts and ideas and make them your reality. By enlisting their help, you're giving them an opportunity to reveal their strengths and participate in your opportunity and its eventual success. And when you help someone climb a mountain, you find yourself climbing higher as well.

SUCCESS BREEDS SUCCESS

As anyone who has achieved it will tell you, success cannot be attributed to luck. Those who enjoy multiple successes follow a common pattern. They know what they love to do and use their experience and expertise to generate new ideas and businesses. Their success is not a game of chance in which they defy the odds, but rather the intentional implementation of success principles that have been employed by legendary thought leaders throughout time. When you apply those proven principles, success inevitably breeds success.

Learning to recognize opportunity when it knocks, like the founders did when they had the opportunity to participate in the founding of

Priceline, is a critical key in achieving success. The true mark of success isn't in the opportunity— it lies in what you do with that opportunity.

Opportunity is always knocking. Start doing the right things in the right order, and you'll start hearing it.

CHAPTER 2

OVERCOMING THE OBSTACLES TO ACTION

Action is the real measure of intelligence.
—NAPOLEON HILL

WHEN NAPOLEON HILL SAID THAT "THOUGHTS BECOME things," he was illuminating the fact that anyone who has ever received anything that he or she wanted began by thinking about it. This being the case, why do some people take action on their ideas while others don't? Why are thoughts simply ways to pass idle time for some whereas for others, they are the seeds of extraordinary achievement?

Dr. Srini Pillay, assistant clinical professor of psychiatry at Harvard Medical School, has a unique and valuable perspective on this question. Dr. Pillay is a brain-imaging researcher who has studied the brain for more than seventeen years in a laboratory at McLean Hospital, Harvard's largest psychiatric hospital, consistently voted one of the top three psychiatric hospitals in the United States, where he also served as director of the Outpatient Anxiety Disorders Program.

As a result of his extensive time spent in clinical work and research, Dr. Pillay also started a company called NeuroBusiness Group, a first-of-its-kind organization that helps people both within the corporate world and outside of it overcome psychological obstacles and realize their greatest potential, using research-proven, brain-targeted methods. This tremendous company was voted one of the Top Twenty Movers and Shakers in Leadership Development in the world in 2013 by Training Industry.

In addition to being extremely qualified to talk about the brain from a professional standpoint, Srini is also a living testament to the fact that thoughts become things, and an expert— from personal experience—at overcoming the obstacles that can stand in the way of that process.

Case in point: When asked how he got to Harvard, Srini replied matter-of-factly, "I called them." It turns out, that's exactly what he did! When he realized that he wanted to go to Harvard, he actually picked up the telephone and called. After asking for the head of Harvard, then the dean, before finally connecting with the head of the Department of Psychiatry, he sent in his curriculum vitae, was interviewed by telephone, and two weeks later got a call informing him that he was in. The rest is history.

Now, it must be said that Srini had done particularly well prior to making that phone call. He was already a top medical student, a concert pianist, a poet, and an athlete. But as he pointed out, there were probably many other people who had similar credentials. The difference was, as soon as he had this thought, he *acted* on it.

He explained that, from a biological standpoint, for an action to occur, the action brain (or motor cortex) has to be activated. To move from idea or thought to action, you have to be committed to the thought, enough to make it a priority.

His commitment came from recognizing that he simply could not stand the situation he was in and needed out. When he fully acknowledged to himself that he really needed to choose where he was going to do his residency in psychiatry, the positivity of making that change outweighed staying stuck in the same old situation in South Africa—so much so that his brain simply caused him to call and leave.

This type of situation, in which you consciously tell your brain why the current circumstance is not good and the future is so much more desirable, allows you to make a deal with your brain to change. In fact, studies show that this kind of "pros of the future" and "cons of the now" approach (what he calls "weigh the play") activates the left frontal cortex and increases both your commitment to change and the chances that you won't just go back to what you were doing. Successful people for whom thoughts become actions always weigh the play. And those who don't do this have a hard time convincing their brains to act.

Yet the question remains: Why do some people act on their thoughts while others don't? As Srini's research has demonstrated, there are in fact quite a few obstacles that can interfere with the thought-to-thing evolution.

The good news is, for every one of these obstacles, there's also an easily applied way to overcome it.

BEGIN WITH THE END

To start out, Srini pointed out an ancient sutra (truism) from *The Yoga Sutras of Patanjali*, which states that desire and its fulfillment are continuous, separated only by time and place. According to Srini, to close the gap between the two, we simply have to nurture the right conditions in our brains to take action.

One of the primary reasons why some don't take action on their thoughts is that they neglect to change their mind-set into the goal mind-set from the very beginning. The moment a successful person has a desire, he or she will start to be-have as the person who has already achieved that desire. For example, successful people who want to be billionaires will start thinking like them long before they have the actual billions in their possession.

Whether you want to become a doctor or a dancer, you have to think, feel, and work like one *before* you become one. It's the only way to get there.

According to Srini, there is plenty of brain science to support this view. Neurologically speak-ing, thoughts are electrical impulses or patterns in the brain. We experience them in words or in images, but they are simply electrons flow-ing around in a circuit. This "thought" circuit has to become connected to the "doing," or action, circuit in order for thoughts to become things. It does this most easily if we imagine ourselves in the goal already, because effectively, our imagin-ings program the brain's GPS with a destination. When that happens, the brain will then map out the route to your destination.

Why, then, do so many people imagine themselves on a cruise but never get to experience it?
Or imagine being in love with the perfect person
but never actually meet anyone? Or dream about
the day when they might lose weight and never
do? According to Srini, it's because there is a
right way and a wrong way to employ the imagination in service of a goal.

Think about expert athletes. Scientists have
studied their brains and psychology for years
and found out some amazing things. When
people imagine lifting heavier weights, they
can. When they imagine swimming, it increases their joint flexibility. The examples
go on and on. But there is a formula for
imagining. People who take action use this
formula, while others give up early because
they lose confidence. Expert athletes rarely
lose confidence, and that is because of the
imagery they are taught to use. Two types
of imagery are best for improving confidence from the start: imagining overcom-

ing adversity or coming from behind, and imagining executing your most feared action (e.g., serve in tennis or putt in golf) flawlessly. It is not the image of holding up the trophy at the end that increases confidence, but the image of coming from behind.

Some people, after gaining confidence, become anxious once they start imagining being on the path toward their goals. So they stop imagining early. Studies show us that the actual image makes a difference. When you imagine in the first person, it activates the brain more strongly, but also causes more anxiety.

To deal with this anxiety, Srini suggests switching to a third-person perspective, wherein you see an actual image of yourself, viewed from outside of your body, in the situation. Imagine, for example, track champions. They, when imagining in the third person, will see themselves lined up at the start line, or running in the track, or reaching the finish line first. In the first person, they will imagine only the track in front of them. Both types of imagery are great for your brain. Starting with third person and then moving to first person can help reduce anxiety.

Srini warns, however, that:

none of this matters if you do not actually believe in your goal. When you believe in your image-thought, your brain will try to mount a response to it. For example, if I asked you to imagine rotating your hand twenty degrees, your brain's action center will fire as if you are actually doing this. But if I asked you to imagine rotating it two hundred and seventy degrees, your brain will simply stay parked. No activation. No action. This is because your brain does not believe that this is possible. When you do not believe that something is possible, your brain does not waste its time trying. That is why my life's mission is to expose people to the science of what is possible in every way that I can.

The bottom line? Those who act dare to imagine, *and* they imagine in a very specific way.

LOSE YOUR DELUSIONS

Procrastination is another common barrier on the thought-to-thing trajectory. Srini explains that there are actually several different kinds of procrastination—arousal, avoidant, and indecisive—and each can be helpful or hurtful.

Arousal procrastinators wait until the last minute to do things because they like the high of the last-minute rush. This can help you when you need the pressure, but it can hurt you over the long haul. You're basically getting a high out of stressing yourself out and, while you may like it, your heart and brain can only take so much of it.

Avoidant procrastinators avoid the task at hand because they can't stand doing it. This can be fine if they don't actually need to do it, but if they do, it becomes problematic. If you have to have a difficult conversation with your spouse, for example, delaying it may only make things worse.

Indecisive procrastinators can't figure out which way to go with an action, so they simply don't, thinking that by not deciding they may never have to act. This may help if you don't have to decide, but what if you do? Someone in a long-term relationship who endlessly delays the decision to marry, for example, runs the serious risk of ending up alone.

To help bridge the distance between a thought and its manifestation as a thing, you have to know which type of procrastination is in your way and find a different way to get the benefit you experience from procrastinating. If you are an arousal procrastinator, find a less harmful way to get a high, such as meditation. In essence, you must replace what activates the brain's reward center so that the reward of procrastination is trumped.

Underlying all of these different types of procrastination are what Srini calls "our cherished delusions." One of these, perhaps the most dangerous one, is perfectionism. People have come to see perfectionism as the gold standard of champions—the secret behind all superior achievement. It's not. In fact, he believes that perfectionism can actually slow the brain down. An extreme example is obsessive-compulsive disorder (OCD), in which people stay stuck in their obsessions and cannot proceed until they are 100 percent sure. Yet even a mild perfectionism can seriously inhibit growth and success.

"If there were one thing I would ask people to lose in order to allow thoughts to become the things that they are," says Srini, "it would be perfectionism. We really need to more deeply understand that champions and successful people are so because they are not stuck in their perfectionism. In addition to being great, they also recover more quickly. If you are someone who falls off the wagon when trying to lose weight, then you may stop trying altogether, instead of breaking down your goal further, or changing it around. If you do fail at reaching your goal, reorient,

reorient, reorient. Recovery involves quick learning, quick self-forgiveness, and moving on. If you want your thoughts to become things, focus on learning the art of recovery. It's as important as being excellent.

"Perfectionism is an illusion that will slow you down and prevent you from ever reaching your goal. When you find yourself being perfectionistic, ask yourself if you are spending enough time in the practice of recovery."

THE FEAR FACTOR

For more than seventeen years now, Srini has studied fear in the brain. He has also seen hundreds of people for whom fear has been a serious obstacle to achievement and happiness. "People think that this is all thought control, and it isn't. The fact is, if we are stressed and afraid, our thoughts will be beyond our control and never become things."

Stress refers to the disturbance of coordinated

brain activity that occurs when, for example, you've had a fight with your spouse, or opened up your in-box and faced impossible requests and demands. People who have this happen to them frequently make a hidden agreement with themselves that their goal is simply to get through the day. They even convince themselves that they have no thoughts about success or, if they do, they have no interest in those thoughts becoming things. If you have this stress and then have to go to a performance review, or visit your in-laws, or meet friends at a restaurant while on a diet, no amount of reframing or refocusing will get you to your goal. In fact, trying to control your thoughts just makes things worse.

So what do you do? One effective option is to practice what scientists call *emotional introspection* and clinicians call *mindfulness*. Simply put, this involves placing your attention on your breath and allowing your thoughts to just be the electricity that they are, without ascribing meaning to them. Do this for twenty minutes twice daily, and you can actually change the way neurons talk to each other in your brain, making your brain much more likely to cooperate in helping convert your thoughts into things.

Another option is to address the stress. The key here is to transform your sense of stress from something vague, overwhelming, and frightening into something concrete and controllable. Figure out exactly what's stressing you—actually write down each item on a piece of paper until you've emptied your head and can't think of any more— take one or two of those things off your plate, if you can, and *then* try controlling your thoughts with reframing or refocusing. Once you do, your thoughts are in a position to be controlled enough to reduce your anxiety (and reduce the activation in your amygdala, or the brain's anxiety center) and then become things.

You also need to make sure you're articulating your thoughts in a way that makes it possible for your brain to act on them. As Srini puts it, "We need to think of thoughts as building blocks. They need to be the right size and shape in order for us to make them into what we want." He goes on to explain that a thought, when it occurs at first, is really an intention, and that there are two kinds of intentions in the brain: goal intentions and implementation intentions. Goal intentions are broad: "I want to lose weight," or "I want to be rich." Those are great starting points, but they are often too large or nonspecific for the brain to actually do anything with them. You have to convert them into implementation intentions in order for your brain to convert them into things.

Rather than a general intention to "lose weight," for example, frame the thought in highly specific, directional terms, such as: "I want to lose five pounds this month by going to the gym on Monday and Friday each week at 8:00 a.m." When you break thoughts down like this, they become amazing building blocks for your goals, and the brain becomes much more cooperative.

Many studies have now proven that implementation intentions are superior to goal intentions in increasing the chances of thoughts becoming things, especially if you mean them and don't just say them. One way to give your intentions more substance is to transfer thoughts from a to-do list to your calendar with a reminder. The brain has so much to do on any given day. Helping it out in this way will really make it serve you and want to help you reach your goals.

Hop That Circuit

If you find that, despite all your efforts, your thoughts are still not making forward progress, it may be because your mind has gotten into precisely the opposite habit—stuck on a circuit of sorts that is keeping you in a rut of nonachievement.

A renowned study conducted many years ago illustrates this phenomenon. In it, a group of psychologists got together to observe the behavior of children and noticed something strange. When the children were in their cribs, they played with their toys and then threw them out. They started to cry. Their mothers would retrieve the toy and give it back to them. They would start to clap and be happy. Then their mothers would turn around, and they would throw the toy out again.

Researchers have termed this type of behavior *retention compulsion*, and it plays out in all kinds of scenarios. There is even some evidence that suggests that we are hardwired for it. When we get stuck in a circuit of disappointment, we simply try to become better and better at disappointment rather than "hopping" to the circuit of fulfillment.

One key mechanism for breaking this cycle is to swing the flashlight of your brain's attentional system from "surviving" to "thriving." This, according to Srini, leads to the *science of possibility*, which is his basic theory, based on years of brain science research and seeing the way in which people behave at the deepest levels.

When converting thoughts into things, he says, you must think in terms of possibility rather than probability—how the *exceptions* have done it, not what most people have experienced. How do people of average intelligence end up with hugely successful careers? How do people who come from abject poverty become wealthy and financially free? Those are the right questions to ask. Saying, "How can I make it when I have these adversities?" will likely cause your brain to freeze and seek to comfort you. In fact, you may never try hard enough because you're afraid to fail.

This lack of effort is called self-handicapping, and almost everyone Srini has seen over the years is trapped within it to some extent. They're afraid to try hard enough because they'll feel foolish if they fail, rather than proud that they tried and got that much stronger and closer to their goal for having tried.

Remember: every practice is a worthwhile trial if you learn from it.

A THOUGHTS-TO-THINGS CHECKLIST

Srini provided a checklist of some of the factors he described above to help you remember what

you can do to increase the chances that your
thoughts will become things:

- Weigh the play to activate the left frontal
  cortex.
- Start with the end in mind to activate your
  brain's GPS.
- Imagine using the specific principles outlined
  above to activate the action brain.
- Know what type of procrastinator you are in
  order to find another way to serve yourself
  and replace what activates the brain's reward
  center.
- Reduce perfectionism to stop your brain from
  stalling.
- Address basic stress before thought control to
  stabilize your amygdala (feeling brain) and pre-
  frontal cortex (thinking brain).
- Control thoughts with attention to breath,
  then use reframing and refocusing to stabilize
  your thinking and feeling brain.
- Use implementation intentions, rather than

goal intentions, to help short-term memory digest information so it can feed it to the action center.

· Circuit-hop from "surviving" to "thriving" by redirecting the brain's flashlight.

· Choose possibility over probability to save brain energy and help it figure out where to look.

Are you serious about allowing your thoughts to become things? Follow these basic principles, and you'll have a great start.

CHAPTER 3

THE POWER OF POSSIBILITY

Your big opportunity may be right where you are now.
—NAPOLEON HILL

IN THE NEARLY HUNDRED YEARS SINCE NAPOLEON HILL penned *Think and Grow Rich*, the world has changed tremendously. From credit cards to cell phones to the computer technology that touches virtually every aspect of our daily activity, human advancements have transformed our lives in dramatic ways and, as part and parcel of that, have had a profound impact on businesses and the products and services they offer.

Given these changes and advances, are the success principles Dr. Hill shared with us nearly a century ago still applicable and relevant in today's business environment? What principles can we pass on to future generations that will stand the test of time and contribute to *their* success?

The cornerstone of Hill's philosophy is that our ability to succeed relies on one thing—thought. No matter what changes lie in store for humankind, that fact will never change. And even though we've experienced remarkable technological advances, achieving success through the power of thought does not necessarily require an earth-shattering breakthrough. Sometimes, the opportunity is already in front of us, just waiting for us to improve it with our thoughts and ideas.

That's exactly what Doug Pick, president and founder of Hearos Earplugs, has done. He saw the potential in an age-old product, one not particularly thrilling on its surface, and through the combination of thought and action was able to tap that potential to create a mega-successful business and the life of his dreams.

Seeing What Others Miss

❖

Doug knew that he wanted to be an entrepreneur at the age of twenty-four. As he contemplated several business ideas and opportunities, one product stood out—earplugs.

> My brother introduced me to the concept of sleeping with earplugs. What I found compelling is that there is a demand and need that won't go away. Earplugs are also lightweight and consumable. As an entrepreneur with a small savings, I had an opportunity to go into a marketplace that wasn't dominated by multimillion-dollar conglomerates.

To him, it made perfect sense, and he launched Hearos Earplugs in 1992. Today, his company is the top retailer of earplugs in the world. According to Doug, the irrefutable distillations of wisdom in *Think and Grow Rich* had a resounding impact on his success nearly one hundred years after it was written. He specifically credits his success on his ability to see opportunity.

In creating Hearos, Doug followed several success principles. First, he kept his mind open to possibilities that the majority of people wouldn't consider. He achieved this by asking himself, "If the trend is to go downstream, what if I go upstream?" His formula for success is to see where the masses are headed, and go the other way.

I have a contrarian mind-set. I am in a business that others didn't see or consider. I can see what's possible, rather than what's already there. I tried to find what is unique, different, and innovative about our products. The forefront of the industry is something that has been around for years. But I saw something that wasn't being done.

A similar principle was employed by Harry Burt Jr. back in 1920. Ice cream and chocolate certainly weren't anything new at that time—they'd been around and enjoyed for years. Then in 1919, the Eskimo Pie was invented—the first frozen ice cream and chocolate novelty. Burt, a Youngstown, Ohio, ice cream shop owner, loved the concept and replicated it in his own store, but his daughter deemed the treat too messy. That sparked an idea. Simply by introducing a wooden handle into the mix, Burt created a portable ice cream novelty that didn't require a bowl or a spoon, and didn't make a mess. Ice cream on a stick was born and laid the groundwork for the Good Humor company, which today is the largest branded producer of ice cream and frozen novelties.

Hill's original interviews showed that some of history's greatest successes were achieved in exactly this way—taking a simple, basic, existing thing and improving on it in some often small way that transformed its usefulness, appeal, and profitability.

How does one turn an existing idea into a successful business that captures the interest and loyalty of the masses? Doug's response is enlightening:

"Sell the sizzle, not the steak, but make sure you have a quality steak."

He found a product that had been around for years, one with a known purpose and value. But in order to attract the market that would make him the go-to for that product, he had to change the way people perceived it. In other words, he had to take earplugs into today's era.

"The key I've found is to not necessarily innovate to the point where you're retraining consumers on what a product might do for them, but to take a product that's already in existence and has demand, add some sizzle, and improve on the quality and the marketing experience."

To do so, Doug went out on a limb and created a business model unheard of in Napoleon Hill's era. There is no signage posted on a brick-and-mortar building packed with dozens of hourly Hearos Earplugs employees. He works entirely from home, has only two employees, and little to no overhead. Yet by utilizing today's technology, he has been able to create a company with worldwide brand recognition that generates a million dollars annually and retails to more than five hundred stores.

And it all started with that greatest of assets: a thought.

Thought + Action: The Ultimate Formula for Success

The success principles shared by Napoleon Hill and the great thought leaders he interviewed are nothing new. People have followed them for decades. Ideas and thoughts are nothing new, either. They've been around since the dawn of man. What is new is how we adopt and adapt our thoughts and ideas to today's unique business climate and challenges, just as Doug Pick did in founding Hearos Earplugs.

However, as the entrepreneurs you'll meet in this book—as well as Hill himself—repeatedly remind us, the key to success is not the thought but the *action* that is taken as a result of it. In the words of Hill himself, "First comes thought; then organization of that thought into ideas and plans;

then transformation of those plans into reality. The beginning, as you will observe, is in your imagination."

Doug is intently focused on his goals, and he is continually finding innovative ways to keep his product and company relevant in a competitive marketplace. He shared the importance of taking action and following through in order to attain success, but, more important, he emphasized that success is directly related to the thoughts that influence us. "Don't hear all the static about why you cannot do it. Only focus on why you *can* do it."

Doug's advice echoes that of Dr. Srini Pillay in the last chapter: to focus your thoughts on possibilities rather than obstacles. Ask yourself "Why not?" and "What if?" The greatest obstacles you will ever face come from making excuses instead of taking action.

How can you apply Dr. Hill's success principles and the offspring of thought as an aspiring entrepreneur in today's business climate, as Doug Pick did?

1. **See possibilities.** Open your mind to possibilities that already exist. How can you adapt an existing product, service, or idea to make it relevant and attractive to today's marketplace? Instead of saying, "That's already been done," ask yourself, "How can I do that differently? How can I do that better?" Keep Napoleon Hill's advice in mind: "Your big opportunity may be right where you are now."

2. **See potential.** See the potential that technological advances have created and how they can benefit your idea. Change is inevitable—therefore, you should stay abreast of current business opportunities and technologies and the advantages they can provide. You can use modern technology to create an innovative business model that enables you to differentiate the way your business is conducted and how you deliver, market, and distribute your product or service.

3. **Take action.** Lack of action has caused the demise of many great ideas and unseized oppor-

tunities. When the seed is freshly planted in your mind, act quickly to give it some sizzle, and you can prevent it from fizzling. This is as true today as it was when Hill said, "Most ideas are stillborn, and need the breath of life injected into them through definite plans of immediate action. The time to nurse an idea is at the time of its birth. Every minute it lives, gives it a better chance of surviving."

4. **Be persistent and patient.** Many successful entrepreneurs adopted Hill's theory that patience and persistence make an unbeatable success combination. Success is not an automatic process. It requires diligence, attention, and the willingness to invest time to perfect your ideas.

Like earplugs, these concepts are not new or innovative. They have been implemented by teachers and students of success throughout the ages and have created groundbreaking businesses. They can be adapted to any idea, new or old, innovative or existing, and are as applicable today as they were a century ago. The principles of business success have not changed; the only thing that has changed is the way we conduct business. Technology and time have opened the door to options and opportunities that we never envisioned before. Notice them. Like a toothpick or an earplug, they've always been there, just waiting for you to improve them through the power of your marvelous mind.

Napoleon Hill observed that "both poverty and riches are the offspring of thought." Which one will your thoughts produce? The answer is entirely up to *you*.

CHAPTER 4

FEEDING YOUR DREAMS

Happiness is found in doing, not merely possessing.
—NAPOLEON HILL

SIR ISAAC NEWTON'S FIRST LAW OF MOTION STATES THAT an object at rest will remain at rest, and an object in motion will remain in motion. This principle is as applicable to thought as it is to every other force in the universe. A mind in motion remains in motion as each thought spawns yet another thought, moving in the same direction as the first.

Thoughts can generate monumental energy and produce results that were once perceived to be inconceivable. Thoughts have led to every invention and improvement known to humankind.

They cause people to become aware of opportunities that would have previously escaped their notice.

And sometimes, the "thing" a thought becomes takes on a life of its own.

Chef Bruno Serato is one individual who has proven the theory that a mere thought, when acted upon, can generate results far bigger and more spectacular than the thinker had ever imagined. Bruno arrived in the United States with $200 in his pocket. He didn't have a job and couldn't speak English. However, he was bilingual, able to speak both French and Italian. He also possessed unbridled enthusiasm and determination, as well as a wide scope of restaurant experience and knowledge. With those assets, he was able to secure an entry-level position as a dishwasher in a renowned establishment, where he impressed his employer with his work ethic and quickly ascended the ranks.

Today, Bruno is the owner and proprietor of the world-famous Anaheim White House Restaurant. His acclaimed entrées, stellar service, and fine attention to detail have earned him numerous awards in the restaurant industry.

But it is Bruno's extraordinary philanthropic acts that have both humbled him and brought him fame, including a knighthood from the Italian Republic and recognition as CNN's Hero of the Year. And while the tables at his restaurant have been occupied by US presidents, world dignitaries, and celebrities, his most important patrons are not his illustrious paying customers. They are the children whose lives he has helped to transform.

The Meal of a Lifetime

~&~

On April 18, 2005, I was walking into the Boys and Girls Club in Orange County, thinking it was a motel. It was actually a residence for children who didn't have a home. I was with Mama, and we saw a young boy eating chips. Aware that those chips might be the only dinner he had that night, my mother said we should give him some pasta. I went back to the kitchen and made pasta for seventy-five kids. That was the first time, but I was not satisfied and started to do it week after week, year after year.

That one thought sparked action and results that have exceeded his expectations by leaps and bounds. Today, Caterina's Club, named after his beloved mother, serves 350 to 400 kids every day, seven days a week. To date, they have served more than half a million meals and counting.

Bruno's generosity is both admirable and incredible. Even more incredible, though, is the fact that no one knew of his mission to feed the children for the first five years that it existed. He didn't talk about it and chose not to solicit funds, assistance, or praise. It was a gesture of love and passion. In his own words, he was "doing it from the heart."

As an entrepreneur and philanthropist, he was providing a selfless service, one without expectation of repayment or reward. He didn't expect to earn fame or receive recognition for his unselfish contributions to the lives of less fortunate children. On the contrary, he was exemplifying true altruism, befitting the legendary Dr. Hill's testament that "great achievement is usually born of great sacrifice and is never the result of selfishness."

Indeed, his achievements are remarkable, but so, too, have been Chef Bruno's sacrifices. Like so many entrepreneurs, the recession took a toll on his restaurant, and his business fell upon difficult times.

"In 2009, I almost lost my restaurant. The economy was 30 percent down, and I was ready to close the doors. My initial thought was that I had to stop feeding the children, not because I wanted to, but due to the economy. But I could not stop my efforts to feed the kids, regardless of the economy. I had to keep going, which made me happier and more confident during the worst economic situation in my life. I feel like I got stronger."

So he persevered, and his business not only survived but thrived. So did his philanthropic work.

SPREAD THE WORD, SPREAD THE WORK

When we're executing an idea that originates from the heart, do we have a responsibility to let other people know what we're doing? For five years, Chef Bruno did not and quietly, without any public knowledge or acknowledgment, he fed hundreds of children every day. In his eyes, it was a selfless service that stemmed from love.

By keeping silent, without expectation of praise or recognition—by not sharing our thoughts and endeavors—we can end up limiting the breadth and scope that our efforts can make. Oftentimes, our efforts trigger the same desire in others who are inspired and want to make a positive contribution to our cause as well. It's all about leverage and the power of leverage when used in a positive way.

In retrospect, Bruno admits he could have asked for help from friends. "I realize the powerful mind that people have as they stepped up to help. I welcomed their help and needed it. Today, I don't pay for the pasta. I receive donations from people who love what I do and want to help. It is great to have that help."

One of the greatest benefits of helping others is what we get in return. While we don't help others for selfish reasons, our acts provide us with an internal reward, which serves as our motive to continue our efforts. When he feeds children, this renowned chef is himself fed by the world's greatest motivator—love.

"The love that the kids give to me is more than I could ever imagine in my whole life."

One thought turned itself into a phenomenal project and a commendable cause that has changed the lives of hundreds of thousands of children. Since that time, the original thought has triggered yet another. Today, Bruno doesn't just aim to put food into the stomachs of hungry children; he also strives to put a roof over their heads. He explained the evolution of this off-spring of thought.

At five o'clock at night, the children leave the Boys and Girls Club and go back to their motel rooms, where they are often exposed to the worst environment possible. I started to investigate the kinds of families living there. Besides the bad ones, I found there are also good families. But because of the economy, they have lost their home or their job and ended up in a motel room. Still, they are hardworking American families. They want to find a job and will find a job. When they do, though, I wondered how they would be able to save the deposit for a two-bedroom apartment. To help each family, I realized I can make a life-changing gesture and pay the first and last deposits for an apartment. In the last seven months, I moved thirty-eight or thirty-nine families, through fund-raisers and donations. We stay behind them for twelve months, and the project is 99 percent successful.

Much like the offspring of thought, the events and experiences in our lives create a ripple effect that inspires our actions. That ripple effect is an underlying reason why Chef Bruno is so passionate about helping these children and their families. Simply stated, he knows what it's like to be poor. Coming from a poor family, pasta was a staple in their diet because it was the cheapest way to feed seven hungry and growing children.

After World War II, Mom and Dad moved to France. The people across the street gave us socks, shoes, shirts, and underwear. I never went to school naked because people donated to me. I do the same thing now.

Bruno's is a classic American success story, and his generosity and determination seemingly know no end. He tirelessly refuses to allow obstacles and challenges to get in his way. Determined to stay afloat during the recession, he even mortgaged his house twice to keep the program running. The key to never giving up, he says, lies in his inspiration.

"If you give up, you give up part of your life. Never give up."

The children are his sole inspiration.

I am not married, but I have three hundred children. The children inspire me.

Obviously, my favorite customers are the children, who are invited to my restaurant. They rarely are exposed to something beautiful like my restaurant. On the day I served my half-a-millionth meal, I invited the children, and invited celebrities and famous athletes to serve them. We asked each of them to do a special interview to provide the children with inspiration to help them know that they can get out of their motel rooms, out of the Boys and Girls Club, and do something special, too.

With firsthand experience in rising above one's circumstances, Bruno can attest to the fact that success is possible for anyone who truly wants it. Through hard work, attention to detail, and a commitment to impeccable service, he has risen from being an entry-level dishwasher to the proprietor of one of the world's finest dining establishments. He followed his passion and built it into his dream by seeing an opportunity and working toward it.

After spending seven years perfecting his craft, Bruno learned that the Anaheim White House was being sold because the owner was not a restaurateur. When he approached the owner and inquired about the asking price, the owner responded by asking how much money he had. The fact was, Bruno didn't have any. But that obstacle didn't prevent him from realizing his dream. He was given the opportunity to rent the establishment for three years, with the option to buy. Literally acquiring the restaurant on a handshake, the deal was based on good faith, trust, and respect.

Today, he passes on similar opportunities to the children he serves in an effort to make a difference in their lives. As he was serving pasta one day, a fifteen-year-old boy approached him and asked if he could work for him. He told the teen that he had to be eighteen years old to work at his restaurant. Three years later, the same young man walked into the restaurant and informed Chef Bruno that it was his eighteenth birthday. True to his word, Bruno gave him a job and his first opportunity to rise above his circumstances and create his own success.

Without a doubt, this renowned chef epitomizes the personal and professional principles identified nearly one hundred years ago by Napoleon Hill. He built a world-renowned restaurant by following his passion, but his professional success provides just a fraction of the fulfillment he receives from his career. Instead, it is the offspring of that business—feeding hungry children—that brings him his true riches: internal satisfaction, pride, and inspiration.

Napoleon Hill speaks of this type of richness

in *Think and Grow Rich*. Often, it is not our professional success, but the offspring of that success, that enables us to carry out our larger purpose. When we are driven by that purpose, it becomes all-consuming and takes on a life of its own.

You, too, have the power to turn your thoughts into something larger than you ever envisioned. When you do, you might find that your original thought was really a stepping-stone toward your true happiness and purpose—the thing you were truly meant to do with your life.

UNLEASH YOUR F.O.R.T.E.

Your forte is your greatest strength or talent. Following Chef Bruno's five-step formula, you can use your forte to set the wheels of success in motion.

1. **Find your passion.** When you find your passion, you'll love what you do and be inspired to use your talents in unique ways.

2. **O**wn your ideas. Your thoughts are yours alone, but to have value, they must become reality. Claim ownership of your ideas and *act* on them.

3. **R**ecognize your opportunities. Chef Bruno followed this principle repeatedly through-out his career. He started with an entry-level opportunity and took advantage of the growth and experience it would provide. He then saw a bigger opportunity to own his own es-tablishment where he could implement his talents and skills to their fullest. Last but not least, he recognized that his business enabled him to pursue a passion that was even greater than his entrepreneurial suc-cess. By joining his ideas with opportunities, he progressed toward his true purpose—the one that brings him his greatest happiness.

4. **T**hink beyond your initial idea. Oftentimes, an idea or thought is just a stepping-stone that can take you even further. Too many people get lost in the details and believe that achieving that initial goal is their ultimate

destination, thus failing to act on subsequent ideas. Chef Bruno didn't have to take it upon himself to make pasta for seventy-five hungry children on April 18, 2005. He had already achieved his professional goals. How fortunate it was that he acted on his idea that day, for both the children and him. That single act took on a life of its own, instilled a new passion and purpose in Bruno, and changed many other lives in the process.

5. Enlist the help of others. Accept assistance when you need it. The greater the cause or goal, the more you will need the goodwill of others. As Napoleon Hill said, "No individual has sufficient experience, education, native ability, and knowledge to ensure the accumulation of a great fortune without the cooperation of other people." When Chef Bruno was at risk of having to stop feeding his "motel kids," he accepted the help he direly needed. Not only was he able to continue with his passion, he was also able to expand upon it.

Napoleon Hill said, "Success in life depends upon happiness, and happiness is found in no other way than through *service* that is rendered in a spirit of love." Caterina's Club has grown exponentially and gained worldwide recognition, with the concept soon to be replicated in Chef Bruno's hometown in Italy. It is the source of his greatest pride—a service most certainly rendered in the spirit of love.

And it all began with a single thought: that one child should not have to go to bed hungry.

CHAPTER 5

MAPPING THE TRANSITION
FROM THOUGHTS TO THINGS

When defeat comes, accept it as a signal that your plans
are not sound, rebuild those plans, and set sail
once more toward your coveted goal.

—NAPOLEON HILL

A MAP IS A RESOURCE THAT CAN BE USED TO GUIDE US to wherever we want to go, whether we're traveling from San Antonio to Miami or we're looking for the best route across town. Using a map, we can lay out the journey from our starting point to our destination. At any point, we can look back at where we've been and how we got where we are today, or set our sights on the future and the places we want to go.

Maps have been developed and utilized for centuries, with the oldest being cave drawings and maps drawn on Babylonian clay tables in 2300 BC. Since that time, maps have evolved and become more complex, illustrating a vast range of data. Today, our ability to access and utilize maps is virtually unlimited. From using printed pieces folded in glove compartments to GPS devices that provide audio and visual directions, we can chart and follow our journey to our destination, both before we embark and after our arrival.

Maps of all kinds have played a central role in the personal development and professional success of Richard Saul Wurman, the founder of TED, a nonprofit organization that provides free knowledge in the areas of technology, entertainment, and design.

Like Napoleon Hill, TED believes in the power that ideas have to change attitudes, lives, and the world. Its mission is expressed through its motto: "Ideas worth spreading," and its renowned TED Talks are viral sensations, many of them racking up millions of views.

Interestingly, Richard is also a cartographer, credited with creating the Access city guides, which provide graphics and information to make places understandable to visitors. Today, he's using his cartography experience in innovative ways. His newest initiatives include 19.20.21 and his Urban Observatory project, both of which revolve around electronic urban cartography, establishing standard methodology for comparative data and live connected urban observatories around the globe.

Though these two career paths may seem disparate, they are in fact both natural extensions of Richard's passion for maps and, more specifically, his unique view of what a map essentially is and the critical purpose maps of all kinds serve in our lives.

"My self-definition of a map is M.A.P., Mankind's Ability to Perceive. A map is a fundamental way to visually understand something. If a map does not work, it's not a good map. It's a performance measure of graphic design. But a map is a treasure. And many people's understanding of a map is different. Many people think Google Earth is an information map, but it doesn't contain much information. It can't show comparative patterns of land use. It's simply a picture."

In fact, Richard has had five careers in his life, virtually all of which have revolved around increasing understanding and providing clarity. He is passionate about maps both literal and figurative, and our ability to map virtually anything, even things we cannot see, such as the human brain. In a speech to the Harvard Graduate School of Design, he spoke of five people he knew who were trained in architecture and how radically different their lives were, as a way of illustrating the fact that we all have different journeys—different maps—even to destinations that may seem the same. "As we are taught, we are like a silo. We start as a private and end as a general. There is a continuum of success."

PERMISSION TO BE INTERESTED

Despite the enormous amount of knowledge and understanding Richard has both acquired himself and spread through his work, he believes that his ignorance is his greatest asset, a belief fostered in him from a young age.

Richard didn't come from what he refers to as a wellspring of academia. His father made cigars, while the other side of his family was poor. But his family gave him permission to be interested in things. When different subjects came up during family conversations, you were expected to contribute and know what you were talking about. He carries that responsibility with him to this day, and it is reflected in all that he does.

"Two words we use often are the words *information* and *question*. I'm interested in that part of the word *information* that is the key part, which is *inform*. And I'm interested in the key part of the word *question*, which is *quest*. I'm interested in the informed quest. Most quests are not informed. We think everything is information. Very few things are really understandable, but I want to understand something. That is my only quest. Historically, if I make things understandable, others seem to, too."

While his accomplishments are many and impressive, Richard points out that he was fired from all but two of his past jobs. He is well aware of his limitations, among them what he describes as "fundamental laziness," which he counters by telling everyone what he is going to do well before he starts. It's just one example of his fascinating ability to understand his own motivation and inspiration. That same depth of understanding is what he attempts to facilitate through TED Talks and his innovative mapping concepts.

Napoleon Hill wrote, "We refuse to believe that which we don't understand." Richard has spent a lifetime gaining understanding of himself and his many endeavors and, as a result, has seen opportunities where others haven't, and created success in a multitude of enterprises and businesses. Through TED, he is igniting that passion for understanding—and its resulting benefits—in millions of others.

Pursuing the Informed Quest

Richard has also had failures, but he has consistently refused to allow them to hold him back. Instead, he uses those experiences to grow and gain an even greater understanding of both his strengths and his weaknesses, realizing the truth in Napoleon Hill's statement that "every adversity, every failure, every heartbreak, carries with it the seed of an equal or greater benefit."

You must not allow any failure to minimize your confidence and prohibit you from setting your thoughts and ideas out on the path to reality. You must not allow it to consume you, for if you do, it will build an impenetrable barrier that will become stronger than you or your thoughts.

Instead, learn from those experiences that didn't have the outcome intended. Ascertain what went wrong and what can be done to avoid repeating it as you move forward. When you can view your failures objectively, you see what a gift they truly are, and you're able to seize them as an opportunity to gain understanding that will improve the likelihood of your future successes. The seed of an equal or greater benefit will then be able to grow—the more you allow it to grow, the stronger it will become. Eventually, it will become larger and stronger than the initial failure from which it sprouted.

This process becomes easier when you adopt Richard's concept of "man's ability to perceive." You'll be able to pull up to the ten-thousand-foot level and view your life as the map it is. You can trace both your failures and successes, see the detours that stalled your progress or have taken you away from your intended goal, as well as the steps that brought you closer to it. Then, with greater certainty, you can correct your path and get back on track toward your desired destination—the transformation of your thoughts into things. And, like so many journeys we undertake in life, that destination will very often exceed your expectations.

TED Talks are a perfect example. What began as an idea to create a convergence among the technology, entertainment, and design industries has become a worldwide sensation. No advertisements or publicizing were used to help it grow. Its success grew from an observation, which planted a seed of thought. From there, the seed flourished into a fully realized vision larger and greater than the initial conception.

SIMPLIFY TO GROW

Richard's success isn't based on coming up with ideas that are bigger and better than the last. Instead, he simplifies his ideas and thoughts, subtracting from them until they are reduced to their most basic form. As a result, his thoughts' journeys to things are completed with fewer challenges, complications, and possible deterrents.

Thoughts do indeed become things, every single day: new products and services, new businesses and concepts and discoveries. And they follow a logical trajectory from point A to point B.

Each of us must have the ability to perceive this trajectory, weed out those that stifle or redirect our progress, and replace them with thoughts of perseverance, accomplishment, and achievement. This is just as true whether you want to start a business, create a software program, or turn your financial state from one of poverty to one of wealth.

Some call it a map, while others call it a plan. Whatever *you* call it, don't overcomplicate your journey or let thoughts of fear or failure deter you. You, and only you, are in total control of your success journey.

Begin by controlling the thoughts that accompany you, paying attention to the steps you take along the way and noticing where they lead you. It is through the "informed quest," not the blind pursuit, that, like Richard Saul Wurman, you will pave the path to your ultimate success.

CHAPTER 6

THE ORIGINS OF THOUGHT

Cherish your visions and your dreams as they are
the children of your soul, the blueprints
of your ultimate achievements.

—NAPOLEON HILL

THE WRITING OF *THINK AND GROW RICH* WAS PRECEDED by twenty years of interviews with corporate leaders and visionaries who, still to this day, rank among history's most successful entrepreneurs. Isolated and analyzed in great detail by Napoleon Hill, the secrets those masters disclosed to him then remain supremely relevant today because then, just as now, the origins of every success can be traced to one thing: a thought.

But how do you *create* the thoughts that lead to successful endeavors? Do you need a business degree to generate viable ideas and bring them to reality? Is it what, or who, you know that ultimately determines where you can take your thoughts, and where your thoughts will take you? Do you need a solid foundation in the industry, or can you be on the outside looking in and create a vision that will have just as much impact?

In speaking with the many entrepreneurs featured in this book, it became clear that the origin of thought is unique to each individual. Some people are naturally gifted with an ability to see things differently. Others are creative inventors of thought, people with vivid imaginations, those who are not willing to accept that the status quo will suffice and those who see an unmet need or unsolved problem and find a way to answer it.

But there's one point on which all these leaders agree: Thought alone does not determine success. It's the *action* taken as a result of that thought that creates real results.

When an actionable thought hits you, you know it—and it can happen at any time. You could be reading a book and get an idea that motivates you to act. A simple observation could generate an idea that inspires you to take action.

Sometimes a great idea comes in the middle of the night and hits you so suddenly and mightily that you bolt out of bed and grope around for a piece of paper and a pen to jot it down, for fear it will be gone by morning.

For David Neeleman, the cofounder of WestJet and JetBlue airlines who is now charting new territory in Brazil with Azul Brazilian Airlines, the best ideas consistently come to him in a very specific time and place.

"I think of things in the shower—that's my time. I think about it, and I can't wait to get out of the shower to make it happen."

Some of the things David has "made happen" during the course his extraordinary career have been quite amazing, a fact he attributes to his unique way of looking at the world.

"How do I go from a thought to something that becomes a reality? I don't think it's luck. I have a lot of deficiencies, but I do have the ability to take a situation and look at it completely different, say that it can be done another way, and ask why it can't be done differently. Then I make it happen."

People who work with David often say he makes it look simple. His reply? "It *is* that simple. It's as simple as one, two, three. Do that and get it done. It's the ability to create something in your own brain. . . . You have to think through every single aspect of it and create it in your brain, maybe as many as one thousand different aspects of it. . . . You have this picture in your brain of what something will be, and you have to somehow paint that picture to investors and people who can help or work for you. You get them to believe in it, and with their help, you create it. People ask me if I'm surprised about the success of JetBlue, and I say no. It's exactly how I thought it was going to happen."

If you're looking for a motto to motivate you through your workday—or your next shower—David's straightforward recipe is one well worth trying: "Think about it, think about it, problem solved, make it happen."

Prepare for Problems, Plan for Success

＞—＜

Of course, no matter how clearly you can picture an outcome or how determined you are to make it happen, you will invariably encounter obstacles on the journey from idea to reality. Like all great entrepreneurs, David has amassed a reliable arsenal of weapons to help him combat and defeat the challenges that arise as he pursues his goals.

One of those weapons is actively seeking out mentors—from his past and his present, through personal acquaintance or through books—whose advice, experience, and expertise inform and inspire his own thoughts and actions. "My father taught me throughout life the importance of treating people equally, regardless of stature. I've had mentors and a lot of people who inspired me to do better and be better."

Another is to always search for a way to simplify a challenging situation, rather than further complicate it. The effectiveness of this approach is illustrated in the way David dealt with an issue that presented itself to Azul Airlines.

"We have 128 airplanes that spend the night in one hundred different cities. One percent of the time, there will be a mechanical problem with an airplane. As the only airline that serves sixty of those cities, we had to figure out how to get parts in to repair and maintain our planes. We had both a logistics problem and an expertise problem. We bought a small, private plane and revamped it as a charter plane that also serves as a mechanic's plane. We manned it with two expert technicians who fly in at night and serve as our centers of excellence, going to the planes and repairing them, instead of having mechanics in every town. We are bringing Muhammad to the mountain, instead of the other way around."

Desire is also a key that keeps David progressing toward his goals, in spite of the obstacles. He doesn't pursue goals he isn't passionately invested in achieving, and that passion helps him keep his eyes on the prize, whatever barriers may arise along the way.

As he puts it, "The challenge is big, but the opportunity is bigger."

David also credits the role his faith played in forming his ability to believe in his thoughts and ideas to the degree necessary to overcome the obstacles that may stand in the way of his success.

> My religion and living Christian principles play a big part. . . . I think [some] people tend to look at everything from a one-dimensional perspective. When you believe there are other dimensions, you can look at it from an eternal perspective. If a business fails from that perspective, in the eternal scheme, it means nothing. There are arguments about God and if He exists, but I believe there are other dimensions. I think when we get back to the faith analogy, we always say, "Pray as if it all depends on God and work as if it all depends on you." You have to get up and do it yourself and make it happen.

Just as critical as developing a plan for defeating challenges is the ability to learn from them when they do get the best of you. It's one of the hallmarks of all great success stories, and David's story is no exception:

When I was in my early twenties, I started a little travel agency. I started with absolutely nothing and was trying to sell timeshares, but they weren't selling, so I was renting them. Then I started putting airfare with it. I was then making good money and hired people to help me. Life was good. Then all of a sudden I got a phone call from the airline I was working with and was told they were out of business. I had customers who had prepaid tickets, and I couldn't pay them back. So my company went out of business.

For some, it would have been a career-ending setback. David chose to embrace it as a powerful learning opportunity that enabled him to move forward smarter, wiser, and better prepared.

That time was my own little depression. From that minute forward, I never relied on anyone else. We started JetBlue, but we raised money to do it. I didn't want to roll the dice again where I had to rely on anyone else.

VISION + COLLABORATION

Do you need a formal education to be successful and make a difference? Is it necessary for you to amass significant experience in a given area in order to create the kind of thoughts that will generate success in that area at a high level?

In fact, some of the greatest successes of all time—David's among them—have been achieved without either.

I have a high school diploma, to go along with my honorary doctorate degrees, but nothing in between. I also have nine children, and five are college graduates. I am a great believer in education, and I think one of the great differences between our country and other countries is the access and ability to get an education. It changes people's lives. I love education and am enormously involved in it. But I don't have a college degree.

He also built three successful airlines even though he is not a pilot and has never flown a plane. He found that working his way up from the bottom and learning the industry and its various trades wasn't necessary. The ability to originate thought and take action, pushing through and past challenges, helped him create his visions. Ticketless travel was one such idea.

I noted that physical, hard copies of tickets were necessary for car rentals and airplane travel. The tickets were like nonnegotiable instruments—if you lost them, you were in trouble. As I watched rooms full of people stuffing tickets and mailing them out, one of our workers asked why we didn't just send a bar code instead of tickets. The idea then came to me that we could just send a confirmation number. But we didn't have a relational database or system to make that work. So I put my partner to work and asked him to create a relational database. As an incentive, I bought him a new Jeep.

Like Trey Urbahn, David also discovered early on that the ability to create success depends on help from others. He invites ideas and the advice of people who have the expertise he lacks, and knows that his success would not be possible without them.

I couldn't have gone to Brazil and started an airline by myself. I handpicked individuals in every area—finance, promotions, marketing, management, maintenance, pilot training, etc.—and offered them founder's shares to help me get the company off the ground. Without that nugget, I would have owned more of the company, but I wouldn't have had as valuable or as big of a company.

By working and collaborating with people and sharing the story of your vision, others will come on board and help you. If it's a great, well-thought-out idea, people will beat a path to the door to support it, be it with their talent, time, or money, increasing both their success and yours in the process.

THE ROAD TO REAL RICHES

Many people hear the title *Think and Grow Rich* and immediately connect it with the idea of acquiring material wealth—and countless followers of Hill's philosophy have done exactly that.

Yet, interestingly enough, Napoleon Hill doesn't

devote a lot of time in his book to the actual making of money.

For Hill, *rich* had a different meaning or, at the very least, a much broader one. Riches, in the context of Hill's philosophy, are the abundance of rewards that inevitably result when you harness and activate your thoughts in order to achieve your goals—they are not the goal itself.

Through his approach to work and life, David Neeleman has grown rich in the truest sense of the term as Hill meant it. JetBlue and Azul have created tremendous financial wealth for him, so much so that he doesn't have to work. Yet he does . . . not for the money, but for the opportunity to help others. "My definition of wealth is happiness and bringing happiness to other people. 'Rich' to me means creating a company that changes the most lives possible and leaves the world a better place."

That is what inspires David, what stimulates his mind to continue generating great thought, and what keeps him motivated to manifest those thoughts through action.

Thoughts will come and go. Businesses and entire industries will come and go. Motivation and desire are what ultimately determine success and inspire entrepreneurs to generate new goals and take action toward them. Like David, when you define your "why," the "how" will appear through inspiration, faith, and collaboration. And so will the riches . . . of *all* kinds.

CHAPTER 7

EFFECTIVE EMOTIONS

One must marry one's feelings to one's beliefs and ideas.
That is probably the only way to achieve a
measure of harmony in one's life.

—NAPOLEON HILL

THE MIND HAS AN AMAZING CAPACITY TO STORE, PRO-
cess, and give birth to our thoughts and experiences. But there is one part of the mind that can
quash our desires and efforts: the subconscious.
This is the portion of the brain that protects us. It
remembers everything that has caused us pain or
regret and recalls that information when we are
in a position to encounter a similar experience.

For instance, if you burn your hand by touch-
ing a stove as a child, your subconscious remembers the pain of that incident. Forever after, every
time you get close to a stove, or anything hot for
that matter, it pulls up the experience and brings

it to your awareness in an effort to protect you and keep you from incurring the same pain.

The subconscious also files away emotional pain: regret, embarrassment, and shame. It's the reason why, when we fail at something, we are reluctant to attempt it again. The subconscious pulls up the memory and uses it to keep us from experiencing another failure and, thus, the feelings associated with it.

While emotions have the power to diminish our drive and negatively impact our chances of success, they can also add strength and momentum to your desire to transform your thoughts into things when you encounter challenges, naysayers, and internal doubt. It is our feelings that keep us from giving up and giving in—even when the subconscious reminds us that we could fail. Indeed, they are the fuel that motivates us to keep pursuing what we want.

Positive or negative, your emotions have a significant influence on your outcomes. The stronger the emotion, the greater the influence. And the more aware and in control of your emotions you are, the more power you have over exactly what their effect will be, and whether it will move you closer to or further away from your goals.

One high-profile entrepreneur who has mastered the art of turning his negative feelings into positive assets is Dave McInnis. The founder of PRWeb and Cranberry, he is a testament to the role that emotions play in virtually every aspect of entrepreneurship, and a fantastic example of how to use emotions to your advantage rather than being controlled by them. His is a fascinating story.

From Anger to Achievement

Emotions were at the center of Dave's response to the question, "How can an entrepreneur know if an idea is viable and will have a chance at success?" They're also a common theme in the creation of his thoughts and the business model he employed.

For PRWeb, I was angry. I had sent a press release out to a company, and nobody cared. It was 1995, and my press release didn't move the needle at all, so I started PRWeb. I had no resources. I used what I had. My total investment was my time and two weeks of initial programming. I also had no business model. For the first three or four years, I didn't know how to charge people. I told people, "If you want to send me money to make you a press release, send me money." It was all based on voluntary donations. By the end of year one, it was $80,000. In year two, it was $1.6 million. I wasn't even charging people. It was money rolling in. When you're getting that kind of donation-based business, you have a certain obligation to delight the customer.

Anger and delight: two powerful emotions from both ends of the spectrum, which Dave was able to tap into and utilize in very different ways in order to create an enormously successful

business, despite the fact that he had no resources, no major investments, and no business
model.

It's important to note that the "delight" Dave
refers to is not his own but rather that of the
customer. He may have had no practical experience, but he had an innate understanding of the
critical role emotion plays in people's decision-
making process. He knew that if he conducted
business in a way that created a positive emotional
connection for customers—if they were *delighted*
with their experience and results—success would
follow. And it most certainly did.

One thing top thought leaders understood
even a century ago is that the greatest success
doesn't come from cutting corners or doing the
bare minimum of what must be done. What has
always set the great apart is their willingness to
go above and beyond—often referred to as "going
the extra mile."

Dave's initial focus on delighting customers
quickly became a fundamental component of the
PRWeb culture: "We hired a man whose job was

to reach out and make sure the customer was happy. Also, every editor had to handwrite at least ten postcards to customers a day thanking them."

By delighting people, PRWeb went the extra mile not just on occasion, but as part of its standard operating procedure. As a result, the company developed not only a powerful reputation but a strong following of fiercely loyal customers.

As the business gained momentum, that customer loyalty was nurtured and maintained through Dave's commitment to continual innovation, which became another vital component of the company's growth. Again, Dave had no experience in this area. However, he explained that he did have good advice.

Paul Allen told me if you're not putting out a press release a month, you're not in business. If you're not announcing that your customer [is] doing something every month, you don't have any momentum. I took that to heart and made sure every four to six weeks we were releasing something new. I also incorporated our strongest users and turned them into our grand advocates. We'd get them on a conference call and preview the product, and they would carry my message for me. They were loyal to the end.

So many people spend time to acquire a new client, but they don't spend sufficient time to keep and retain their existing clients. Successful businesses like PRWeb know that it's more cost-effective to keep existing clients than to spend time and resources continually trying to acquire new ones. A business absent of loyal customers will have a short life span. In the words of Dr. Hill, "Lack of loyalty is one of the major causes of failure in every walk of life."

PRWeb created the kind of loyalty that virtually guarantees success by establishing a positive emotional connection with customers up front, then finding innovative ways to keep them coming back to experience new services that are being offered.

FEAR AS FUEL

Embarking on a business venture of any kind, much less one unfamiliar and unconventional—as PRWeb was at the time—is inherently risky and naturally induces a certain amount of fear. Dave wasn't immune to that fear, but it didn't stop him from launching PRWeb a mere two weeks after he began building it.

> Analysis paralysis comes from fear. Whenever I feel fear, I dig a little deeper because that is where opportunity is. Everybody else has the same fear. With Cranberry, I learned that Google News was doing the same thing, and I thought I'd lost my opportunity. I looked at the analytics and realized Google didn't matter.

So, fear *was* a factor, but in this case, a positive one. According to Dave, the greater the amount of fear, the bigger the opportunity. In fact, he uses fear as a sign that his idea has real merit and great potential—an attitude that hearkens back to Napoleon Hill's declaration nearly a century ago: "Fear is nothing but faith in reverse gear! The foundation on which both faith and fear rest is belief in something."

Fear wasn't an impediment after he sold PRWeb and was looking for another opportunity. That's when he founded Cranberry, his second very successful business.

I played around for a couple years and was looking for an entryway back into the press release space. After doing some work, I decided there was no opportunity and it had run its course. My whole reason for existing was to create media bypass opportunities where we didn't have to rely on the media to carry a message for the client. We are now hiring journalists to interview clients and write stories. Then we drive traffic to that story and market it. We are news marketers.

It was another foray into uncharted territory—and another enormously successful one, thanks to Dave's already-proven emotion-driven formula of finding an unmet need, offering something better or different than what is already available, and delivering it in such a way that the customer will gladly pay for it, even if he doesn't have to.

What are the emotions that surround your dreams and goals? Positive or negative, they can impact your thoughts and, consequently, your results in profound ways. Cultivate the ability to acknowledge your emotions, take control of them, and direct them toward positive, productive actions that move you closer to the achievement of your goals.

CHAPTER 8

CONQUERING THE MOUNTAIN

*There are no limitations to the mind
except those we acknowledge.*

—NAPOLEON HILL

JUST AS DAVE MCINNIS SET OUT TO DO SOMETHING HE
had never done before, and was able to climb to
the top with no resources or experiences, Werner
Berger has stood at the bottom of a mountain,
defied great odds, and come out on top—in his
case, both figuratively and literally.

From his humble beginnings in a three-room
farmhouse without electricity or running water,
Werner rose to become an international corporate leadership consultant and the founder and
president of Strategic Results International,
which focuses on creating collaborative, vibrant
workplaces. He is also an expert in human po-

tential. His accomplishments and feats are many, not the least of which is holding the record for being the oldest person on earth to have climbed the highest peak in each of the world's seven continents.

As it turns out, the same set of principles has enabled him to scale such great heights both on land and in business.

IT ALL BEGINS WITH ATTITUDE

When preparing to climb a mountain, Werner has a very clear and compelling set of objectives.

I know the consequence of my actions— the cost of doing and not doing. Does the mountain care if I worked my butt off to get fit? No, only my teammates and I do. After years of pushing myself physically, I don't have the same passion for working out. So what? The mountain doesn't care. The only question—"Do I wish to make the top and get back safely?"—I decide. As long as the perceived rewards—emotional, spiritual, and/or financial—outweigh the personal cost, I give myself no options. Work out, or quit the quest. It really is that simple. Do or don't do. You choose!

Unfortunately, I have experience with many who have said, "I choose to do," and then don't do anything. This saddens me, since they have just deceived themselves. It's perfectly okay to "not do." It's not okay to say yes and then not do. You are, or are not, your word. I have also learned, the moment I truly become my word, my life changes. What happens is a shift in *beingness*. I urge, pray, and challenge everyone to step into this life-changing declaration. It's a decision that takes a split second and transforms everything.

Climbing the highest peak on each continent is so challenging that few would undertake it. Even fewer would complete the task, finding it too difficult and monumental, and giving up too easy and convenient. Such goals require tremendous mental preparation and conditioning—the same type of conditioning that one must commit to in order to succeed at any goal.

Dr. Hill said, "One of the main weaknesses of mankind is the average man's familiarity with the word *impossible*." Werner certainly had ample opportunity to give up on his goals because they seemed too impossible to achieve—but he didn't. What kept him motivated and determined was a positive attitude that didn't accept quitting, even when the going got tough. He says that from his experience on the mountains of the world he has concluded that "attitude is everything" as it relates to an enjoyable and successful climb. His three attempts at reaching the top of Denali (Mount McKinley) provide a great example of this.

On my first attempt, a woman from England was part of our small group. Her reason for being on the mountain was to prove to her male banking partners that she could hold her own against the "boys"—not a good reason to be on a mountain that has already claimed over 120 lives. On one occasion, as we approached a steep section of the climb, she blurted out an obscenity, and said, "Do we have to climb that?" My thought: *Yes, that's why we are here, isn't it?!* Needless to say, she dropped out about halfway through our twenty-four-day adventure. We, too, did not reach the top, since we were literally blown off the mountain only two hundred vertical feet below the summit by high-velocity, gusty winds, and clouds starting to obliterate the terrain. We escaped being trapped up high and got back to high camp, three thousand feet below, just before midnight.

The second time we got stuck at the same high camp. This time, the group was larger. Unexpectedly, a blizzard moved in and kept buffeting our tents and dumping tons of

snow on us for nine days. On occasion, we
had to get up more than once a night to
shovel snow off our collapsing tents. During the day, we reinforced each tent by
building double snow-block walls around
each enclosure . . . soon again to be eroded
by the punishing winds. Within our team,
we had some very mixed feelings about the
situation. Some attacked the chores with
energy and vigor, made snow sculptures
in white-out conditions, played competitive
games, and wrote and/or read in our snow-
bound enclaves, while a few others desper-
ately wished to be somewhere else. By day
five, a serious state of lethargy had set into
the latter group, to the point of real con-
cern. They became pale, showed signs of
altitude sickness, and hardly ventured from
their sleeping bags. All they could think of
was the warmth and safety of home, whereas
the rest of us were praying for a break in the
weather and the final chance at the sum-

mit. Instead, the weather gods presented us with a small weather window, just enough to escape down.

These situations taught Werner two critical lessons:

We chose to be on this mountain—we had to expect potential adversities. When the adversity occurred, we had the option of thinking neutrally or negatively about it— neutral thoughts allowed for positive actions, whereas negative ones led to negative feelings. These feelings culminated in adverse behavior, and, of course, physical, mental, and emotional deterioration.

They also cemented in Werner's mind the essential correlation between attitude and results. "Change your attitude, change your results, change your life!"

THE CLIMB NEVER ENDS

No doubt, Werner is an active person. His physical accomplishments would be astonishing even for a much younger man. The progress he's made from his childhood home and life to the success he has gained in business took a great deal of commitment, attention, and time. These feats don't come easily—you cannot be a bystander to your own success.

With so much activity, progress, and involvement in his goals, it's easy to understand why Werner had difficulty when he sold his company.

At age forty-three, I sold off the company, ostensibly retired, and promptly died—in an emotional sense, that is. You see, I had gone away from, and not toward, something. A year later, I lost our family's wealth, first to an 18 percent mortgage rate and next to the stock market crash of 1981. In the meantime, my ex had started her own successful

business while I became the househusband.
It did not take long for "housewife syn-
drome" to kick in . . . doing the same thing
over and over in a never-ending cycle of
nonappreciation and nonfulfillment. Two
years later, I was an emotional basket case,
taking on the most mundane jobs to simply
get out of the house. I had to find something
challenging, something to inspire me.

It took another two years for Werner's next
breakthrough to arrive.

I had the opportunity to join a consulting
group, which became my lifesaver. Like
crazy, I studied functional coaching mod-
ules and people skills, designed by the
Wilson Learning Corporation, drew on all
of my past experiences as a company owner
(and chief cook and bottle washer), and
gradually assembled a trusting client base. I
graduated from consulting in customer
service, to consultative selling, to manage-

rial excellence, to high-level leadership, and ultimately training trainers in thirteen different technologies. After four years, I had found home. Gradually this group of nine highly effective, self-employed consultants dwindled until I was the last one to leave. I was generating a lot of business and had still been hoping for a miracle. Three months later, the firm declared bankruptcy. I was in the final stages of a divorce and had left almost one million dollars of business on the table, yet my emotional well-being and my life had rarely been better.

In 1982, I was a participant in the Werner Erhard EST training. The facilitator asked us to think of three things we'd love to do before we died—something we'd probably never do. The movie *The Bucket List* had not yet provided us this moniker. What came to mind was "climb Kilimanjaro and the Matterhorn and hike to Mount Everest Base Camp." Two years later, my adventurer son, Paul, asked me about going to

Everest Base Camp. I jumped at it, and in 1992 we found ourselves in the magnificence of the Nepal Himalaya, and me, at the beginning of a newfound love affair (or passion). Once again, I was reminded of the magnificence of all creation and, in awe and with humility, I bowed to the magical wand of the creator. Since that time, I have now become the oldest person on earth to have climbed to the highest point on each of the seven continents (including Mount Everest), have been to the top of Mount Kilimanjaro four times, and continue to lead transformational leadership expeditions to remote and magical places.

Werner has mastered the art of perseverance against the odds. Throughout his life, he had to reinvent himself in order to accomplish his goals. It's no small coincidence that he was honored with the first-ever Life Reimagined Award. Like Dave McInnis, he acknowledges that there were times that he was indeed afraid—but he didn't allow that fear to stand in the way of his objective. He simply kept going.

Fear has not played much of a role in my climbing. And this does not mean I am never afraid—even though I might hide my fear, especially from myself. For years, I allowed my early conditioning to have me be self-conscious (actually, unconscious), wishing to be invisible. I had no sense of self. I thought of myself as shy, never realizing this was simply a condition of my mind and me not owning who I am. In retrospect, I still ask myself, "How can anyone not have a sense of the true magnificence of self?" Ultimately, that's all there is in life.

On the mountains, unexpected situations are expected. In those moments, the only question is, "What needs to be done now?" It's always about what's next and never about "woe is me." There simply is no time for that. No payoff. While true in many circumstances, especially on the mountains, this strength of character might evade me in interpersonal situations. My tendency is still to fight or flight, and counteracting either slams me right back into my commitment to being my word, even in the mirror.

THE VIEW FROM THE TOP

Attitude, action, and commitment: In listening to Werner recount the ups and downs, challenges and victories, of his life, these are the character traits that shine through. They're the traits that have helped him rise in life, against the odds . . . and what empowered him to turn his thoughts into things and his ideas into record-setting awards.

Yet for Werner, as with so many of our other entrepreneurs, success is not just about an achievement, an award, or a title. It is defined by the way he lives.

Success, simply put, is having your health, loving your life and the people who surround you, and enjoying the contributions you are making in the world. To that, I would add: freedom to do what you love and having enough money to support that.

Having accomplished both personal and professional success, one would think that there aren't many goals left on Werner's bucket list. But for this consummate doer and achiever, the horizon is ever expanding. His next pursuit? Launching a global peace initiative. Ultimately, he wants to be remembered for more than the records he has set. He wants to make a difference in the world.

I want us to be remembered as the instigators that led to a global shift in thinking and a welcoming of all conflicts being resolved through goodwill and collaboration. We can't continue to live in a dog-eat-dog world where competition reigns, religious differences lead to a license to kill, poverty is exacerbated by wanton arms spending, and environmental damage is inflicted in the name of progress, and then expect a happy and prosperous future.

Asked to offer some words of wisdom for other aspiring entrepreneurs and adventurers, Werner shared his conviction that success at anything, large or small, is possible for anyone, but that it requires true interdependence among families, friends, business relationships, societies, and nations. In other words, whatever mountains you may climb in life, there will be times when you need to reach down and help someone else up on our way, and others when you need someone to give you the mental or physical strength to get to the top.

Just remember that as long as you have a positive attitude and extend that attitude outward, it doesn't matter how you take the next step. The object is to keep moving, one step at a time.

CHAPTER 9

SILENCING THE CRITICS

*Put your foot upon the neck of the fear of criticism
by reaching a decision not to worry about what
other people think, do, or say.*

—NAPOLEON HILL

FEAR IS A FOUR-LETTER WORD THAT CAN HAVE A DEVAStating impact on a business. However, a certain level of fear is healthy—it keeps us from throwing good money after poor ideas. Sometimes it makes us back up and examine our reasons, purpose, and plan more closely to gauge whether we're willing to take the risk. A healthy dose of fear can actually help us make better decisions.

But how does fear affect people entering unchartered territory and those who have pioneered the unknown in order to aspire to their dreams and goals?

Let's step back in time to the 1940s. World

War II dominated the news, and millions of men registered for the draft. In the same decade, McDonald's opened its first restaurant in San Bernardino, California. The Jeep and Superman also made their debuts. Morton Salt came into our kitchens, and synthetic rubber tires were introduced to our cars. The Mark I computer was invented in 1944, followed by the first electronic digital computer, in 1946. Physicist Harold Lyons built the world's very first atomic clock and, on the lighter side, we learned that everyone loves a Slinky and just how fun Silly Putty can be.

In the same decade that introduced penicillin as a cure for diseases, another historic path was being carved in the medical field—one that has both helped and inspired many to pursue non-traditional medical treatments and careers, and reap their remarkable benefits. That path was carved by a female pioneer, Dr. Gladys Taylor McGarey.

Dr. Gladys has been practicing medicine for more than sixty years. She was the first doctor to utilize acupuncture in the United States, has broken ground in natural childbirth, and is known across the globe as the Mother of Holistic Medicine. Today, she is the cofounder of the American Holistic Medical Association and the Academy of Parapsychology and Medicine. She is also ninety-three years old. Hers is a success story of historic consequence.

THE "HOW" WILL COME

Dr. Gladys always knew she wanted to be a doctor, even though it was extremely rare for women to enter the medical field. After all, back in the 1940s, the role for most women was housewife and mother. Few worked outside of the home, and far fewer ventured into nontraditional careers that were once reserved by society for men. Her aspirations sent her into largely unchartered territory.

How did she overcome the obstacles that certainly presented themselves during the process?

What went through her mind and motivated her to follow the unbeaten path by venturing into the medical field before women were accepted with open arms? Her extraordinary story contains lessons we can all benefit and draw inspiration from, even today.

Since I knew from age two that I had to become a doctor, it was not something I had to decide. I just had to decide how I was going to make it happen, and stick to it. Knowing that I was to become a doctor gave me the strength to face the obstacles that presented themselves. They were irritations and sometimes stumbling blocks, but they were never stop signs. Since I was severely dyslexic, my challenge was an internal one, and the obstructions from the outside were things I would just have to deal with when I was faced with them. I had to learn how to take things as they came along and deal with them the best way I could.

Dr. Gladys had confidence in herself and great belief in her life's purpose. Perhaps the greatest fear she faced was that of criticism. After all, she was a woman entering into a male-dominated field. According to Dr. Hill, the fear of criticism "is almost as universal as the fear of poverty, and its effects are just as fatal to personal achievement, mainly because this fear destroys initiative and discourages the use of imagination." To conquer it, the motivation must be greater than the fear. They are both powerful emotions that have the potential to move us forward or hold us back.

For Dr. Gladys, motivation trumped all and kept her moving ever forward toward her goal, drowning out the voices of criticism, disapproval, and doubt.

THE MIND/BODY CONNECTION

However, she is quick to acknowledge the profound impact that emotions can have on our health and the importance of staying in tune with what's happening at the emotional level.

"Forgiveness is huge. I need to forgive myself and others so that I can get on with life. The word tells us what to do. We can thank it for giving us the opportunity to experience whatever that life lesson was. This may take years, and we may never completely accomplish our goal, but the path is much healthier and more pleasant than hanging on to resentments. It becomes like a scar that has healed, instead of a sore where we are always picking off the scab."

Dr. Gladys believes that the opposite of love is not anger—it is apathy. "Anger is energy and sometimes is very appropriate. If it goes blind, it becomes hate and that is a killer. If it gets stuck, it can cause disease. But apathy stops all movement of energy and stops the flow of life. Nothing good can happen when apathy is in control, no growth, only decay. It takes away the light and moves into darkness."

As a highly successful, internationally renowned doctor, Dr. Gladys has seen the benefits of healing not just disease and the body, but also the mind and spirit. Her vision of an integrated East/West approach to wellness has many aspects.

> It is blending the art and science of medicine—reclaiming the feminine face [compassion] of medicine. It allows the life force, or spirit, to be active so that Life Itself becomes the healer. It is claiming life, understanding that we deal with diseases, but are not those diseases. In the long run, love is what does the healing. Eastern and Western modalities are just different ways of practicing the art and science of medicine, and they blend very nicely if we give them a chance. It is like moving into the light.

Dr. Gladys likes to say that she is "ninety-three and prescription-free." She is certainly a rarity there, and the treatment methods and methodologies she has pioneered have contributed to her outstanding health and longevity. To her, it's about taking control of one's own self and embracing the freedom to make the choices that are best for you.

If I find that a prescription is indicated at some time and I decide to take it, I can tell it to do the work it knows how to do, and leave the parts of my body which are working just fine alone. I acknowledge it as a helper; I do my own healing.

The fact that the mind is so powerful that it can actually heal the body is fascinating—and absolutely in line with Dr. Hill's "thoughts are things" philosophy. Though she has applied the positive power of thought to experiences such as natural childbirth and treating diseases, Dr. Gladys readily acknowledges the impact of thoughts on broader issues, including happiness and professional success.

Thoughts are living things which create other thoughts, which are living things.

They are also magnets. They attract like thoughts and like thinkers. The thoughts which are created come from what we let our thoughts dwell upon. What is our Ideal? What do we have to live for? What do I want to get well for? I, personally, choose to dwell in gratitude.

In other words, if our thoughts are of good health and well-being, we will produce just that—in *all* aspects of our lives. If we dwell on what we want, those thoughts will actually attract and create the living counterpart. The same information shared by Napoleon Hill in *Think and Grow Rich* can be applied to business, success, happiness, and, as Dr. Gladys's life's work demonstrates, even our health.

FROM PRIVATE BELIEF
TO SHARED DREAM

Obviously, the mind is a powerful vessel. Not only can it give birth to thoughts, it can inspire and motivate us to pursue them. It has the ability to change the outcome of virtually every aspect of our lives if we pay attention to it and give it permission to do so.

So how do we move that power outward? As a doctor, how does Dr. Gladys convince her patients that her techniques have merit and will benefit them—even when they may not share the same belief?

If I have an idea and I don't know what another person thinks, I may just dangle that idea out there and see if the person latches on to it, rejects it, or ignores it and respond to their response. If I think it is an important concept and they don't accept it, I may just bring it up again and again until they think it is their own original idea. Mission accomplished. Most of the time an argument doesn't accomplish much. Reframing is often very helpful, but if it is important, I don't give up.

The lesson? Not everyone will agree with an idea—but that doesn't mean it isn't worth pursuing. If it is an important concept, it should be pursued, time and again, if necessary.

Dr. Gladys used these principles to become a pioneering figure in the medical field, and she did it without the fear of criticism. It's a principle she teaches in her practice as she helps people heal the body with the mind. In doing so, she has made history while making a positive impact on thousands of lives.

Your thoughts are living things—capable of changing not just your life, but the lives of countless others. It is your responsibility to nourish your thoughts from infancy, protect them from the external forces that would harm or even destroy them, and bring them to maturity so they can have a magnificent life of their own.

CHAPTER 10

THREE FEET FROM GOLD

What we do not see, what most of us never suspect of existing,
is the silent but irresistible power which comes to the rescue
of those who fight on in the face of discouragement.

—NAPOLEON HILL

IN THE SAME DECADE THAT DR. GLADYS WAS ENTERING the medical field to save lives, World War II was claiming lives. Some fought in the battle and survived. Others didn't engage in the war but, nevertheless, fought for survival. The victims of the Holocaust had their own battle wounds, ones that took a toll on them both physically and mentally. Those who were in concentration camps had to rely on an inner resolve to endure the realities of being held captive—a resolve based on faith but cemented by strength.

Steven Spielberg's Oscar-winning film *Schindler's List* depicted the scenes that many prisoners of the

Holocaust experienced every day. The tales of survival embedded in their memories are examples of strength and perseverance that prevailed even in the most brutal situations. Jack Beim is one of these survivors. Jack's quiet demeanor speaks of grace and dignity, but his words tell a tale of amazing fortitude and strength that surpasses the average person's comprehension.

SURVIVING ON HOPE

Jack was a boy when he became a prisoner. One of his first memories is of the selections being made, separating the prisoners into lines that would seal their fates. Because of his age, he was deemed useful and categorized as a worker. However, his father and younger brother were placed into a different line. Knowing what was going to happen, his father pushed his younger son into another line, with the intent to save his life.

Every day, Jack was forced to perform grueling physical labor, but two things gave him the strength to carry on. One was hope; the other was his brother. Too young for such physical toil, his brother was kept behind. Food was sparse, to say the least, and his brother risked his own safety and well-being to hide a piece of bread to give to his older sibling. The familial loyalty and unselfishness helped Jack endure the bleakest of times.

During his years in concentration camps, Jack was beaten frequently. His observation skills grew keen after witnessing a daily killing ritual. Soon, he learned to observe where the shots were coming from and where they aimed, and he ran in the opposite direction. With no sign of impending liberation, hope hung by a mere thread—but it was hope that saw him through the horrible conditions and experiences he was exposed to during his imprisonment. When asked how he did it—how he endured the hunger, pain, and brutality—he replied, "Hope. I had a chance . . . if I stayed alive."

It was well known that escaping wasn't an option. While the prisoners outnumbered the guards, the guards were heavily armed. Their dogs would find whatever their bullets missed. Those being held in the camps had only one choice—to stay in the camp, do what they were told, and hope that they would live long enough to experience freedom. For those still on the outside, the choice was just as clear. The only way to avoid imprisonment or death, the only way to survive, was to hide.

Such was the case with Jack's wife, Adele, who was just five years old when she became what was known as "a hidden child."

One day, without warning, Adele was sent to live with one of her father's clients. After her grandparents were taken out of the house and shoved into trucks, her father took her to another family to keep her safe. Originally, the family was asked to keep her for a couple of months. Those months became three years. A church found another home for her brother. Like many

Jewish people, Adele and her brother remained hidden. Not allowed to go to school, she also couldn't go into town or see her family. During house searches, she was hiked up and hidden between boards in the house, shaking with fear and—though she was only a child—fully aware that if anyone learned that she was Jewish, she would be killed.

Naturally, Adele missed her parents and family. Initially, she spent many nights crying. Yet she was aware that when she was in hiding, she couldn't cry or make any sound whatsoever. Like the prisoners in concentration camps, she knew that her survival required her to accept her conditions.

Traumatic experiences leave emotional scars. Those scars revealed themselves when Adele was able to return to society, her family, and school. After the war, she was the only Jewish child in the school, and an eight-year-old child just entering kindergarten. To help her adjust, her parents put her in the Montessori school system, but still, she felt like a lesser person than others. She was timid and shy, with a fear that others would not like her for being Jewish, understandable given the circumstances of her early life. This insecurity and inferiority complex took time to overcome. Feeling "less than" is not easy, but she now counsels others who suffer from the same feelings to be stronger and love themselves.

After many decades, Adele understands that trauma does make one stronger, and it makes her appreciate what she does have. Throughout the years, she and her husband have shared their individual experiences of survival with their children. It has been their goal to provide them with a happier life than they had. That goal has been accomplished.

The survivors of the Holocaust can all give us a lesson in hope. There was no end in sight, no date marked on the calendar that would signify the end of being held captive. Liberation was not certain. It was merely a wish—the one thing that saw them through one more hour, one more day, week, month, and year.

Keep On Digging

Chances are, none of us will have to endure the kind of unimaginable ordeal Jack and Adele faced in their young lives. But all of us go through tough times when we're tempted to accept defeat, and must dig deep to find inner strength. It's easy to lose hope during difficult times. When success is not a certainty, sometimes we cannot see beyond our immediate challenges and imagine the possibility that our goal, our dream, may actually exist.

Far too many people have never experienced success, simply because they give up too soon. In fact, the majority of aspiring entrepreneurs who do give up do so when they're closer to a breakthrough in their success than they've ever been. They just don't know it.

During the historic American gold rush of 1849, thousands of prospective miners traveled to San Francisco to claim their stake to the rich fortune that was buried beneath the ground in what would later become the state of California. As in nearly every worthwhile endeavor, success was not a certainty and it required hard work and patience. The forty-niners, as they were called, found that mining wasn't easy—the job was tedious, difficult, and often dangerous. With a pick and shovel, they'd dig into the ground in the California sun from dawn to dusk. Their only encouragement and motivation was hope.

It was no secret that it would take time. None of the miners thought they'd strike gold on the very first try. But few were prepared for the fact that their efforts would take months or longer. Inch by inch, the work was grueling, with no reward or pay. Eventually, the miners would resign themselves to the fact that their efforts were futile, and they'd either move on to a new location where their prospects might be better, or they'd quit altogether.

Thus, gold mining gained the reputation of being a "try and fail" pursuit. Try and fail, try and fail, try and fail again. It was those individuals who were willing to fail as often as necessary that eventually succeeded. Those who packed up their shovels when they failed went away empty-handed and disillusioned with their dreams. Little did they know that the longer they kept at it, the more likely it was that they'd succeed. Their reward—the gold they'd come so far for—was within their reach, just a few "feet" away, when they gave up. They could not see past the present moment and the possibility of success. As a result, they lost hope.

Remember what Jack said about hope enabling him to survive the concentration camps: "I had a chance . . . if I stayed alive." The miners had a chance, but only if they didn't give up hope. The same principle applies to any endeavor you undertake. The moment when success seems impossible is precisely when you have to find the inner resolve, strength, and fortitude to keep going. For it is at that moment that you are closer to success than you've ever been.

Just because you cannot see liberation around the corner, it doesn't mean that it's not going to happen. Just because you haven't yet struck gold, it doesn't mean that it's not there. With just a little more digging, you'll find it. But first, you must dig up the strength to keep on trying. You have a chance, but only if you keep your dreams alive.

The mental and emotional strength to overcome challenges and obstacles is a prerequisite to success. There will always be challenges and there will always be obstacles. In the end, those things will have less impact on your success than your strength to overcome them. When you replace doubt and disappointment with perseverance, strength, and fortitude, you will find a way to turn your thoughts, ideas, and goals into reality.

As Napoleon Hill said, "Thoughts mixed with definiteness of purpose, persistence, and a burning desire are powerful things."

CHAPTER 11

FAILING TO SUCCEED

Opportunity often comes disguised in the form
of misfortune, or temporary defeat.

—NAPOLEON HILL

WITHOUT A DOUBT, FEAR OF FAILURE CAN TRANSCEND
into reality. After all, thoughts do become things.
Whether it originates in the skepticism of others
or is the result of periods of difficult struggles,
fear can be quite real and cause many to give up.
Some may not try at all, while others may find
themselves tempted to give up too hastily. They
lose the initial hope and motivation that spurred
their idea and resign themselves to impending
failure.

Remember, though, that the fear of failure is
just a thought, and it's not the thought that matters most—it's the action you give that thought

and the perspective from which you see it. It's the offspring of the thought that will have the greatest impact. For instance, if fear of failure triggers a stronger desire to overcome obstacles, one will try harder and likely make progress. On the other hand, if the thought of potential failure instills so much fear that one is afraid to take any action at all, failure is inevitable.

This chapter examines fear from a new and quite different perspective as we explore the possibility that failure can be a positive element in one's eventual success. This principle has been proven throughout history among some of the greatest entrepreneurs, including those interviewed by Dr. Napoleon Hill. Let's take a look back through history and re-familiarize ourselves with them.

The great Henry Ford wasn't a stranger to failure. Before founding Ford Motor Company, Ford's earlier business endeavors all failed and left him broke. One of the greatest artists of all time, the famous Vincent van Gogh, sold only one painting during his entire lifetime—just one. And we cannot omit Thomas Edison, who failed in his quest to produce a lightbulb thousands of times. Edison understood that failure was not a negative—in fact, he perceived his unsuccessful attempts as positive steps toward success, as reflected in his now-famous quote, "I have not failed. I've just found ten thousand ways that won't work."

Those are just a handful of failures experienced by highly successful entrepreneurs. They are joined by Colonel Sanders, whose Kentucky Fried Chicken recipe was rejected an astounding 1,009 times before being accepted by a restaurant. R. H. Macy had seven business failures before Macy's department store found its initial success in New York City. Walt Disney was told he lacked imagination and had no good ideas. After several business failures, he filed for bankruptcy. Even after Disney became a success, he was met with skepticism and criticism and was told that nobody would pay money to see a cartoon mouse. Today, the beloved Mickey Mouse has outlived his creator, and Walt Disney's parks, movies, and books have generated billions of dollars of profits.

Taking our tour of failures into the modern-day era, best-selling novelist Stephen King received thirty rejections on his first novel. That novel, entitled *Carrie*, eventually became a mega best seller and a major motion picture. Sony's first product, a rice cooker, was a total bust, as was Bill Gates's first business, Traf-O-Data.

What do these entrepreneurs have in common? They didn't give up, even after facing rejection after rejection and multiple failures. Like Edison, they knew that each so-called failure brought them one step closer to their ultimate success. The mind-set of these highly successful entrepreneurs intrigued me, so I wanted to see how the possibility of failing might impact aspiring entrepreneurs in their first quest for success. That's when I met Nick Evans, the coinventor of Tile.

Tile is not a new concept—it helps people locate their lost items. Nick Evans found an opportunity to make it smaller, affordable, and available to more people. You simply attach it to an item and turn on your phone to find your item. The beauty of the device is that it enables the user to utilize the technology from other people's phones, thus extending the range and the number of people who are actively seeking to find the item. If someone has a Tile on their bike and their bike is suddenly gone, they launch the associated app on their smartphone and hit a button that says their bike is lost, and the smartphone of every other Tile user in the world would begin looking for the bike. This technology is not new—but Nick and his partner, Mike Farley, saw an opportunity to put it together elegantly and make it run off a small battery.

To get started, they obtained a financial investor, but they also used another source: crowd funding. They put together a campaign with marketing material and generated a great deal of interest. They were even able to purchase advertising prior to manufacturing by getting firm quotes and knowing the economics of their product. In other words, they did their homework.

I asked Nick to share his definition of failure and how failure impacted his experience.

That's a hard one to answer. It really depends on how you look at it. The whole valley [Silicon Valley] has a different take on failure. People somewhat embrace it, but they understand that failure is on the path to success.

That's a fascinating concept. Silicon Valley depends on innovation and constant inventions and changes to technology. Without failures, these inventions would not exist. In developing and launching so many new products and technologies, though, there is certain to be some degree of failure. Because of that, it is necessary to acquire the mind-set that failure is acceptable and a vital part of creating ultimate successes. In this environment, it is not feared but rather considered to play a positive role in innovation.

Dr. Hill told us that "strength and growth

come only through continuous effort and struggle." Still, given a choice, it's understandable that
most innovators would prefer success over failure. We would prefer our path to be smooth,
continual, and free of barriers or detours. The
reality is, however, that we will encounter set-
backs and obstacles along the way. If we know that
there are bound to be challenges in our pursuits,
how can we stay motivated and on track without
becoming discouraged or disillusioned? Nick
Evans offers this advice:

> Take the lessons that you learned and try
> it again. It's hard to do sometimes. It's es-
> pecially hard to do because of the outside
> pressure—because of your own thoughts
> around failure. If you're embarrassed to tell
> people you're going to try to do this and then
> you don't succeed, and then now you have to
> face that, it's natural to think you need to
> stop trying so hard and putting yourself out
> there or that maybe you need to be a little
> more conservative and get a normal job.

Everyone might not jump on your bandwagon and think your idea is credible. Nick admits that people thought he and his partner were crazy, but they've proven them wrong. "You really have to believe in yourself. You have to understand that even if you do fail, it's still okay."

Because the creators of Tile saw new things on the market that made an existing idea better and viable, they were able to tap into a huge market. By adding the shared searching technology, they've created an extra component to their app that could offspring onto other apps. In other words, their invention could become a model that is used by others in their products. This brings us to another fear—the fear that exposing our ideas to the public could result in their being stolen, borrowed, or copied. It is a possibility, but according to our entrepreneur, it's one that should motivate, not stop, us from pursuing our vision. "That's an indicator you're doing something right, when people are starting to follow your lead."

Tile is a new product that is enjoying impressive success, even though its creators had little to no experience running a business. They weren't aware of the potential obstacles they might encounter; therefore their fear factor was very low. What they did have, in place of fear, was a vision and a strong belief in it, even though their technology was not new.

These two gentlemen are not alone. Others have also created success based on existing products or services and have done so because they believed in their vision. A contributing factor to their success is confidence—in themselves and their idea. Without confidence, they would have been more likely to listen to critics who thought their idea too risky and offered well-intentioned advice not to quit their day jobs.

NFL Super Bowl players Jacoby Jones and Thomas Smith weren't recruited by a single college. They got their "breaks" as walk-ons. They were willing to take a chance because they believed in their potential. It is entrepreneurs like these who end up turning their ideas into realities—people who are willing to take risks, face potential rejection, and push through that rejection.

Fear is a natural part of the success process. To overcome fear, you may have to make a conscious effort and become aware of its presence and potential impact on your goal. Above all, you need to see your fears as healthy signs and turn failure into opportunity. The next time fear threatens to interrupt your vision, ask yourself these questions:

1. **What am I afraid of?** Are you afraid of criticism, rejection, or failure? Identify the source of your fear and you'll likely see that you can handle rejection, criticism, or failure.

2. **What's the worst thing that can happen?** Your fears are imaginary—and even if they do play out, your imagination likely turns them into something greater than they really are.

3. **How can I use my fear in a healthy way?**

Like our entrepreneur, you can use fear in a positive way, seeing it as a sign that you are, indeed, on to something big. Let it motivate you toward your goal.

What if you do experience failure in the pursuit of your goals? First, realize that you're not alone. In fact, you're in very good company. The greatest thought leaders and entrepreneurs of all time have failed. What set them apart is that they learned how to apply each failure to their future success. Ask yourself these questions when you encounter obstacles or experience failures:

1. **What went wrong?** By identifying what doesn't work, you are one major step closer to finding what does work. In this case, failure is a good thing!

2. **How can I correct my course and achieve my goal?** Take a lesson from professional navigators. When a pilot encounters turbulence, he does not turn around. When a captain

sails stormy seas, he stays on course. They realize this is a temporary situation and they must keep their eye on their destination. Turning around or abandoning ship is not an option.

3. **How can I use this experience in a positive way?** Often, obstacles and failures provide us with answers and solutions that will reveal where we need to go and what we need to do to overcome them. Let them motivate you as you realize that they've brought you closer to the success you want to achieve. Find the opportunity within the experience to turn it into a positive, and you'll be more motivated and inspired than ever in making your ideas the realities they can and should be.

CHAPTER 12

LEADING BY LIVING R.I.C.H.

*It is literally true that you can succeed best and
quickest by helping others to succeed.*

—NAPOLEON HILL

SOMETIMES, LIFE'S GREATEST OPPORTUNITIES ARRIVE
when we least expect them. At those moments, we
have a choice. We can retreat into fear and un-
certainty, giving in to our own doubts and the
discouragement of others. Or we can rise to the
challenge, making the choice then and there to
accept the destiny that has been presented to us,
and summoning the resources to be worthy of it.

When Dina Dwyer-Owens was thirty-five, her
father's death left the services company he had
founded, The Dwyer Group, without a president and CEO. Dina was asked to fill his role—a

request that was not unanimously supported by everyone in the organization. She knew that others expected her to fail—in fact, they told her so. Faced with skepticism over her lack of experience and knowledge of the industry, she had to quickly prove herself and win the trust and confidence of others.

Agreeing that she lacked experience, Dina requested that they give her six months to prove that she was capable of doing the job and doing it well. She may not have had executive experience, but she was a customer and knew what customers wanted. That was the knowledge she was bringing to the table, and it ultimately created massive growth in their business.

Today, with more than thirty years of experience and a string of phenomenal successes to her credit, Dina is still serving as CEO and chairwoman, overseeing seven franchise brands with more than sixteen hundred locations around the world. She was the 2012 Ernst and Young Entrepreneur of the Year for the Southwest Area

North, and was featured in the very first special episode of *Undercover Boss: Epic Bosses*.

The foundational values of the company she took over, along with Dina's own personal values and her conviction that there is always room for improvement, have formed the cornerstone of her impressive success.

A Foundation of Riches

While building and maintaining a profitable business is always Dina's primary goal—one she's proven exceptionally good at achieving and exceeding—it's not her only goal. Equally important to her is making a meaningful impact on the lives of others, especially as she endeavors to help others create success in the ownership of their franchises.

Her commitment to that goal is the natural extension of her father's founding vision and legacy. The Dwyer Group was built on a code of values based on his business beliefs, which he codified so that they could be implemented on a day-to-day basis and be used by employees to hold themselves and one another accountable. This code is known internally as Living R.I.C.H., an acronym for Respect, Integrity, Customer Focus, and Having Fun in the Process, and has become a centerpiece of the company's identity and branding.

The effectiveness of this code was tested, however, with Dina's *Undercover Boss* appearance. Her mission on the show was to pose as an employee in one of her own franchises, in order to find out whether the core values she and her father had worked to instill were, in fact, reaching their frontline staff and enhancing their customers' experiences. While being on the show often exposes bosses to negatives in their business, Dina embraced it as an opportunity to identify what was working and find ways to improve what wasn't. Her observations helped her reinforce the Dwyer Group brand and keep it alive.

PRIORITIZING POSITIVITY

Positivity is another important factor in Dina's success. Her definition of the offspring of thought is "the power of positive thinking," and creating and maintaining a positive environment and spirit in the workplace is one of the hallmarks of her leadership. In her experience, the benefits of such an environment are manifold:

- Performance is higher in positive environments than in negative environments.
- Being positive results in higher sales.
- Positive people are more resilient and, therefore, better able to overcome challenges and find solutions.
- Positive people have less stress and make better decisions under pressure.
- Positive people can see beyond the problem. They have a broad perspective, which enables them to see solutions and implement changes when necessary.

To help her maintain positivity in her business, she is an avid student of motivational, inspirational, spiritual, and educational CDs. Outside the workplace, she turns to spirituality for strength and to gain and maintain the confidence necessary to operate as a high-level executive.

As part of that commitment to positivity, Dina also counsels aspiring entrepreneurs and leaders to strive for authenticity—to understand who they want to be and what their true goals are, instead of trying to model the goals and paths of others. In that same vein, she urges people to do what they love and to hire others to cover the aspects of the business they don't enjoy or aren't good at.

As she says, "If you don't do what you love, it will be torture. It should be one of those things where it doesn't feel like work."

Through helping others create successful businesses, Dina Dwyer-Owens and The Dwyer Group understand the meaning of living "rich" as Napoleon Hill understood it—the meaning he strove to promote in *Think and Grow Rich*. Their vision is driven by values, not profits, and their business is extremely profitable as a result. Their success is totally dependent on the success of their employees and franchisees. As a result, success is enjoyed by all. Each of their franchises is based on an original idea, with service at its center, and their growth and sustainability can be attributed to remaining aligned with that idea and with the values that helped their organization.

Most people seek to create wealth first and expect that a rich and rewarding life will follow. The opposite strategy is the one you should adopt. When you live authentically, pursue your passion, and seek to support and enrich the lives of others in the process, those values will ultimately create the material wealth you're seeking. It's the strategy at the heart of Napoleon Hill's philosophy. It worked for Dina Dwyer-Owens and The Dwyer Group. And it will work for you, too.

CHAPTER 13

FROM TRAUMA TO TRIUMPH

Great achievement is usually born of great sacrifice,
and is never the result of selfishness.

—NAPOLEON HILL

OFTEN, THE SEEDS OF OUR GREATEST TRIUMPHS AND breakthroughs are planted during our darkest hours and most challenging moments.

For Michelle King Robson, founder and CEO of the women's health website EmpowHER.com, that time came when, at the age of forty-two, she underwent what she would later discover was an unnecessary hysterectomy, then endured nearly a year of unanticipated pain and suffering as a result of it.

Michelle experienced moments of true despair during those months. She even contemplated ending her own life. Yet in the midst of this crisis, something happened that would eventually change not only her life but millions of other lives all over the world.

"At my lowest point, I made a deal with God. If I could get better, I would make sure no other woman had to suffer the way I did. Not on my watch. Not if I could help it."

After crisscrossing the country in search of a doctor who could provide an explanation of and relief from her symptoms—and receiving neither—Michelle sought out answers on her own, everywhere she could, including, of course, the Internet.

I posted on the Web continually, saying, "I'm depressed. I've had a complete hysterectomy. Can somebody help me?" I was looking for a woman like me. Someone who'd walked a mile in my shoes. And it was crickets. I probably posted to two hundred websites, all these sites saying, "We can help you. Talk to us." I never got a response.

Finally, at the urging of a friend, she read a book by a doctor whose philosophy resonated with her, and whose practice also happened to be in her own backyard. She made an appointment and started a protocol of two simple treatments that, in just five days, did what eight months, twelve specialists, and nine pharmaceuticals hadn't been able to do: get her better again.

With her health restored and her mind cleared, Michelle set out to make good on the promise she had made. "I got sick. I got well. Then I got MAD. And you don't want to get a woman mad, because she's going to run out and start a company."

Michelle knew firsthand that there was a huge, underserved population of women who were flocking to the Internet with questions about their health and wellness. She also knew that what they were looking for wasn't there.

She could see clearly what she needed to create: a content-rich, easy-to-navigate website where those women could find the information, answers, and support they needed to make better choices and have more control over their health and lives—in other words, the exact resource she *didn't* have when she was sick and searching.

The question, of course, was how to create it. That question took time, trial, and error to finally answer.

"IF YOU BUILD IT, THEY *WON'T* COME"

At first, Michelle freely admits, she didn't know what she was doing. "I wasn't an Internet person. I wasn't a technology person. I never went to college. All I knew was, I had passion and I had resources." What she needed was, as she puts it, "the right people in the right seats." But like many new entrepreneurs, her initial instinct was to fill all of those seats herself.

I thought it was so easy. *Oh, I can build a website, no big deal. Everybody's building a website.* The problem is, nobody's going to come. You have this thing called Google. And Google doesn't want to rank you in the right way. Just because you're a company that serves women, that has good intentions, doesn't mean they're going to find you. You have to have people who are experienced in certain areas on the Internet who can help you get that list that you need . . . who understand search engine optimization . . . who can create content every day.

Ultimately, Michelle discovered the enormous power in one of the simplest acts of all: *asking.*

I asked someone, "Who can I get to help me do this?" I hired somebody who is my right-hand man, who actually knew what he was doing, because he came out of the start-up world and technology. And he's the one who created the first website.

Michelle continued to implement her asking policy until she had assembled a team of experts who had the skills and knowledge to bring her vision to life and make EmpowHER a viable Web presence. Her passion for asking even extended to the details of the site itself. She was adamant that EmpowHER include an "ask" button that would allow people to submit specific questions and receive a timely, informed personal response—a goal she fought for over the objections of some of the very experts she had sought out to help her.

They said, "You can't do that. You can't have an ask feature. It's not a scalable model." I had no business experience. I didn't care. I said, "I don't know what the hell a *scalable model* is. It's what I want and it's what you're going to provide because I'm paying for it. So you go figure it out."

They did, and today "Ask a Health Question" is the site's most popular feature.

DEBUNKING THE
MAGIC-BULLET MYTH

⇥⇤

Michelle is quick to warn aspiring entrepreneurs not to buy into the myth of the overnight Internet success story. Even after assembling the right players and giving them the room to do what they did best, it took time to get EmpowHER to where it needed to be in order to have the presence and level of impact she had envisioned.

There's no magic bullet. There's no magic pill that you can take to get this to work. I've learned that through time. It's hard work and it's putting forth a hard effort and it's having everything in it . . . you have to believe in yourself and believe in what you're doing and believe in your team.

She also advises those thinking of starting their own businesses to be "ruthlessly focused" on their goals and objectives. "Do one thing and do it well. That's it. Not ten things. One thing and do it well. If you don't do that, then you're not going to be successful. You're taking your eye off the ball."

More than six years later, all of the hard work, time invested, and lessons learned have paid off. EmpowHER is one of the top five women's health sites on the Web, and one of the top seven health sites overall, with tens of millions of unique visitors each month. Michelle has been rewarded for her vision, hard work, and commitment with awards, accolades, and, most important to her, feedback from countless people all over the world who say that the site she built has enriched, improved, and even saved their lives.

THE CHOICE TO *ACT*

Michelle was fortunate enough to have read Napoleon Hill's *Think and Grow Rich* at a young age. She says those principles have stood the test of time and stayed with her—particularly Hill's insistence that it's not merely thought, but thought wedded to *action*—that produces results.

"[An idea] starts as a seed in the brain. From there, you have to decide what you're going to do with it. Are you going to execute on it or are you going to keep it in the brain and keep it a seed? Lots of people sit around and talk. Talk is cheap. If you want to do something, get off your ass and get it done."

Michelle's choice to act on the promise she made to herself and God during her darkest hours has resulted in the creation of a business that is everything she had envisioned and more. Her thought became a thing that has impacted and will continue to impact lives in the most important and meaningful ways imaginable— including her own life.

I have all the passion in the world to make sure that no other woman suffers like I did. It's all about passion. I have the drive and I have the dream. That's what this is about. It's about living the dream.

CHAPTER 14

FINDING IDEAS, FUELING THOUGHTS

All the breaks you need in life wait within your imagination.
Imagination is the workshop of your mind, capable of turning
mind energy into accomplishment and wealth.

—NAPOLEON HILL

ARE WE ALL CAPABLE OF PRODUCING IDEAS THAT CAN transform into reality, or is the ability reserved only for those with certain talents or genes?

To Brian Smith, the creator of UGG Boots, the difference between people who have a great idea and let it go and those who run with it and impact the world, comes down to one word: *vision.*

Brian is an individual who is highly skilled at finding opportunities in unlikely places and turning them into massive successes. He believes that ideas are abundant—they are everywhere we turn if we know how to identify them and are open to exploring even the smallest thought, wish, or idea that sparks in our minds. It's a process that he's witnessed and experienced multiple times. He's seen great ideas transformed into reality and watched as great ideas have been dismissed without any action at all being taken on them.

The first time he experienced this phenomenon was at a noisy party with friends in Perth, Australia.

I noticed [my friend] Richard sitting off by himself, turning over and over in his fingers the corkscrew bottle opener from the wine table. I was intrigued that he seemed oblivious to the rest of us, so after a few minutes, I walked over and asked what he was doing. Surprised, he looked up at me and said, "If I designed this I would have done this, and this and this," etc. Then he put the corkscrew back down and joined the party.

Richard never went into the corkscrew business. But, as Brian saw it, "the difference between him and the twenty or thirty others who used the corkscrew was that he envisioned something that they did not."

That observation taught Brian to look for, recognize, and *act* on opportunity when it arrived.

TAPPING A HIGHER SOURCE OF INSPIRATION

✦

When creating UGG, Brian was guided by a connection to the universe, one that he says has always guided him and, at times, even saved his life. At the age of thirty, he had an unfulfilling career as a chartered accountant, and no idea what he really wanted to do with his life. One day, while listening to the song "Time" by Pink Floyd, which describes the way many people drift through their lives and put things off indefinitely, he had an epiphany.

"I sat bolt upright, and my body became covered in goose bumps (my higher self's way of letting me know I am on the right track). I thought of all my accounting friends who were tracking toward the coveted partnerships and others who were running successful businesses, and realized I had been running in place for ten years. I'd missed the starting gun. I had a strong sense of a voice inside me telling me that the life I was living was not in harmony with what I really wanted."

Through yoga, Brian discovered meditation, which helped increase his state of awareness. During one session, his mind drifted and was filled with random thoughts about businesses and their products. He realized that many of the products enjoyed and used by his Australian friends had actually originated in the United States. Suddenly, he felt a strong calling to come to America, where he would find the next hit lifestyle product and bring it back to Australia. That would be his business—the sought-after answer to what he was meant to do with his life. Less than six weeks later, he was in Los Angeles. Less than six months later, he found the next hit lifestyle product.

While reading *Surfer* magazine, Brian came across an advertisement showing two pairs of legs in front of a cozy fireplace, with the feet clad in sheepskin boots. He remarked that everything about the ad was absurdly out of place in a magazine published in Southern California and devoted to surfing, palm trees, girls in bikinis, beaches, bare legs, and bare feet.

"The ad screamed to me, 'You're going to be a huge success!' I'd been in California less than six months, and here was my future staring back at me from the pages of *Surfer*."

He showed the ad to a friend, who replied that he didn't get it. "Boots," he said. "Who wears boots?"

"Exactly," Brian answered. Nobody in sunny California did! Sheepskin boots were worn in Australia, where sheep outnumber people. But there were no sheepskin boots in America. He reasoned that if even half of 1 percent of all Americans bought sheepskin boots, and he was the only one selling them, he'd be rich.

The voice inside me had been right all along. The problem was that I had gotten its message backward! My destiny wasn't to come to America, find the next big thing, and bring it back to Australia. The next big thing was already in Australia. My destiny was to bring it to America, where I would be wildly and immediately successful.

The next big thing was already there—he just hadn't seen it yet.

THE VALUE OF IGNORANCE

This vision of success is typical of the blind optimism shared by most people during the aha moment when they conceive their new dream. I believe that for a true entrepreneur, some degree of ignorance is a key ingredient for success. If you knew at the time all of the obstacles you're up against, you'd never even start.

This was the case for Brian.

I was totally ignorant of the fact that Americans had little knowledge of the amazing attributes of sheepskin being rugged, breathable, washable, and, above all, comfortable. To them, it was hot, sweaty, prickly, delicate, and good for jackets and mittens—not footwear. For Australians, sheep are such a central fact of life that it's near impossible to get through the day without some kind of dependence on them. If I had realized this culture clash at the outset, I probably would have tossed the magazine aside and gone back to dreaming of skiing the grassy hillsides of Australia.

Brian's first step was to contact the company that had placed the ad in *Surfer*, Country Leather in

Western Australia, to get some sort of exclusive agreement to sell their products in the United States. He called immediately and spoke with Country Leather's owner, George Burcher, who told him he'd had a lot of calls from Americans wanting to distribute his boots.

Brian realized he would have to make Burcher as convinced as he was that he was the right guy.

I told him that, like him, I was a West Aussie, from Perth, and that I was an accountant looking to start my own business. I told him I'd raced in the National Windrush Surfcat sailing championships in his hometown, Albany, and I recounted every other piece of Aussie trivia I could think of to try and create a bond between us.

Ultimately, Brian did get the go-ahead from Country Leather and went to work testing the market. The rest, as they say, is history. By the mid-1980s, UGG Boots were a fashion icon in the United States. Today they are a wardrobe staple for people of all ages from coast to coast.

This sensational success story is the direct result of a thought—or, more aptly stated, taking action on a thought. Not everyone would look at an ad for sheepskin boots and envision them adorning the feet of Southern Californians—we all have different types and levels of creativity. How was Brian able to take an existing product and think of a different way to market or use it?

Thinking is a very personal thing. There are so many types of thinking, it is difficult to define. There is negative thinking and positive. Quick thinking and slow. Right thinking and wrong. Audacious and conservative. To some extent, we have used all of the above in getting to where we are in our lives, and what that place looks like is the sum total of all our combined thoughts. But . . . I have come to the conclusion that my best thoughts come when my intention is not to think. I can't tell you how many times I have been stuck on a problem, or lacking direction, or even seeking inspiration, when the answer has come through meditation.

I usually set some intention prior to relaxing and will have a pen and paper nearby, but then I sit still (in no particular location—I've had some great thoughts on planes), and do my best not to think. Now, quite often, I get nothing, but more often than not, I will get ideas that seem inspired and to me these are the purest thoughts. I'm convinced there is an intelligence in the universe that we can all tap into if we practice. Many people only hear it in times of despair, when they seem to have hit bottom, when the human channel of thought is depleted. But that spark is always there to speak words of encouragement and to give new thought to the genuine seeker.

CHAPTER 15

SETTING THE TABLE FOR SUCCESS

More gold had been mined from the mind
of men than the earth itself.
—NAPOLEON HILL

THE TABLE: IT IS THE ICONIC GATHERING PLACE, THE
ultimate symbol of togetherness, connectedness,
and community. It's where friends meet for conversation and advice and families join together
to share their laughter, dreams, fears, thoughts,
and ideas. The table has been the center of entertainment and recreation in our personal lives,
and the site of brainstorming, planning, trans-
actions, and the exchange of funds, ideas, and
advice in our professional lives.

Entrepreneur Rob Angel found a way to turn
the fun and conviviality of the table into an amazing success. And from the start, he gathered oth-

ers around his own "table"—people who helped him complete, test, and perfect his idea and create a business from it. In fact, you could say his product and idea stemmed from a picture-perfect table.

WHAT YOU DON'T KNOW CAN *HELP* YOU

Today, Rob is a phenomenally successful businessman, the creator of the beloved board game Pictionary. But in 1985, he was a struggling waiter. During a lull, he passed time by picking random words from the dictionary, drawing a picture representing them, and having others guess the word. His colleagues loved it, and what started out as a way to pass the time between shifts at work soon evolved into a bigger idea.

But Angel knew what he didn't know. In order to attract the publicity and interest necessary to make Pictionary a household name, he needed help. First, he needed money in order to print his board game. Family credit through a loan from an uncle provided him with the funds to get several thousand games printed.

Angel had three business partners: his uncle, who was his financial adviser; a graphic artist, who designed the cards and board; and a business partner, who made up for the fact that he was, by his own admission, "an incredibly average businessman." Together, Angel considered them a dream team, providing him with the expertise he lacked in different areas. He also tapped the wisdom of a gentleman who had done all of the printing for the mega-popular board game Trivial Pursuit.

Angel's willingness to bring on others who could fill in his gaps in knowledge, experience, and expertise played a huge role in his ultimate success. He also believed in his product. "Years later, people told me they thought I was crazy, but we kept plugging away. We knew early on we had something special and never looked back."

Yet their success took work—it didn't happen overnight. "We did hundreds and hun-

dreds of demonstrations, and approached re-
tailers throughout Seattle to sell a handful of
games at a time." Department stores ultimately
became their biggest customers, and an order of
167 games from Nordstrom paved the way to Pictionary's success.

In early 1986, Rob's team licensed their game
and started their own game company. In 2001,
Pictionary was so successful and popular that it
attracted offers from major game companies and
was sold to Hasbro.

THE THIRD MIND

The game that millions have played around the
table was successful because of the assistance,
support, and advice that was received from others
with the experience and insight to make it possible. Napoleon Hill referred to this kind of collaboration as the Master Mind group, and he
valued it so highly that he enshrined it as one of

his Thirteen Principles. Hill defined a Master Mind as "a coordination of knowledge and effort, in a spirit of harmony, between two or more people, for the attainment of a definite purpose."

Hill's vision of the Master Mind came from none other than Andrew Carnegie, the steel magnate who joined together with others for one purpose: to create a steel empire. As Hill described it,

> Mr. Carnegie's Master Mind group consisted of a staff of approximately fifty men, with whom he surrounded himself, for the DEFINITE PURPOSE of manufacturing and marketing steel. He attributed his entire fortune to the POWER he accumulated through this "Master Mind."

You may, without realizing it, already be a part of a functioning Master Mind group. Such groups include boards of directors, advisory councils, mentors, financial and business partners, or even just like-minded achievers with whom you connect and exchange ideas on a regular basis.

Whatever name your group goes by, however many members it contains, the benefits are undeniable. A Master Mind can:

- Contribute new ideas and give you important feedback.
- Immediately increase your existing networks and connections, multiplying the number of people who can help with different aspects of your business or plan.
- Open the door to partnerships with people in similar businesses who have invaluable experience to share.
- Provide relevant and quick information that would otherwise take years, or decades, to acquire on your own.
- Keep you focused, on track, and accountable as you strive to turn your thoughts and ideas into a successful business.

There's no denying the value of a Master Mind group to an aspiring, inexperienced entrepreneur like Rob Angel. But they play a viable role in the ongoing success of established entrepreneurs as well. Author J. R. R. Tolkien joined with Charles Williams, Owen Barfield, and C. S. Lewis to create a Master Mind group of writers who together helped him to create *The Lord of the Rings.* One of the most famous Master Mind groups in history named themselves the Vagabonds. Its members included Henry Ford, Thomas Edison, President Warren Harding, and Harvey Firestone of the Firestone Tire Company.

The people who gather around your table collectively create another voice, which Dr. Hill described as a third mind: "No two minds ever come together without, thereby, creating a third, invisible, intangible force which may be likened to a third mind."

Your ability to create things in the world is increased by having that invisible "third mind" of the Master Mind group. Whether the group is assembled to help one specific individual or idea, like Rob Angel's Pictionary, or to help every member of the group enhance their success and grow their businesses, a team of professional advisers with different skills, talents, ideas, experience, and perspectives is an asset to a business.

Rob Angel made his creative genius a household name with the help of others. He needed financial support, skills he didn't have, and expertise in areas where he lacked it. He knew what he didn't know and didn't attempt to go it alone. In acknowledging and accepting what he needed to make his dream come true, then going out and finding those things, he created a team that turned his picture-drawing game into a blockbuster commercial success—proof that great ideas can be created by one, but great successes are created by many.

The next time you gather around the table, tap into the power that's around you. Seek insight and feedback from friends and family, advice from professionals, and ideas and new perspectives beyond your own. When you know what you don't know and turn to others for their invaluable support, doors open, ideas are expanded, and success is accelerated.

With the right people around you, your thoughts will become things much more quickly and easily, and you, too, can create picture-perfect success.

CHAPTER 16

THE COMMON DENOMINATORS OF SUCCESS

*Create a definite plan for carrying out your desire
and begin at once, whether you are ready
or not, to put this plan into action.*

—NAPOLEON HILL

THE AVERAGE PERSON WILL SPEND ANYWHERE FROM fifty thousand to ninety thousand hours working during their lifetime. That's a lot of time to invest if you don't truly enjoy what you're doing.

One of Napoleon Hill's greatest revelations was the critical importance of finding fulfillment and reward in one's work. Most people want to know that their work is appreciated. Even more, they want to know that they're making a difference—that their contribution creates a real benefit, whether to an employer, employee, client, customer, or society. As Hill understood, and as the entrepreneurs profiled in this book have repeatedly emphasized, *that* is the source of true "riches," and most people who pursue it find that it is the prerequisite to financial success, not the result of it.

Like Dr. Hill, Dr. Myra S. White has also studied the impact of thoughts on success. Dr. White is a clinical instructor in psychiatry at Harvard Medical School, and she teaches leadership and strategic talent management at the Harvard Extension School. Like Hill, she researched and interviewed successful people in an attempt to identify commonalities among them. Her work focuses on the implementation of thoughts—the actions that successful people take to turn thoughts into things. In conducting it, she chooses to focus on people who actively prioritize the kind of positive contribution that aligns with Hill's definition of rich.

I'm not interested in who people are, what they look like, or their personalities, just what they do to transform thought into reality. I only select people to study who act with integrity and strive to make a positive difference in the world by adding value to the lives of others either through the products they produce or the acts that they do to improve the quality of people's lives.

Dr. White became interested in this research around the turn of the millennium, when she realized that her career was, in her words, "going nowhere." She had a PhD in psychology from Harvard's Graduate School in Arts and Sciences and a JD from Harvard Law School. Yet while this put her into a small, select group of people in the world, she had never figured out how to leverage her education in a way that would allow her to fully use and express her expertise and experience. Like many people, she wanted to do meaningful work and make a positive contribution to the world around her. Instead, she seemed to be stuck in an endless series of dead-end jobs on the road to nowhere.

This led her to start looking back on her career to find out what had happened to what seemed like a promising beginning.

As I contemplated my path, it began to dawn on me that I had no idea how to succeed in the American workplace. I had come to the United States as a child from England. My father had died before I was born, and my mother decided to remarry an Englishman living in the US who managed a state park, where we took up residence. My parents were never acculturated, and I was essentially raised to be a proper English schoolgirl. The adults who visited our house were primarily English acquaintances and relatives who were traveling in the US. Moreover, no one was even remotely interested in success, personal achievement, or making lots of money.

Her first glimmer of the American world of success and personal achievement came when she met her husband at age nineteen. "A savvy American, he decided that I was cut out for greater things than just an undergraduate degree and became the engineer of my success in academia. He taught me how to write simple American sentences, how to gain admittance to top schools, and then succeed as a student."

Unfortunately, before she could fully launch her career in the real world, her husband tragically died of cancer. Without his guidance, she was lost. Her promising career essentially evaporated.

These thoughts started her on a quest to find out how people succeed and become influential leaders in their area of endeavor. "I wanted to know what the key steps are that people take to create their success. How do they translate their thoughts and desires into effective action? My goal was to identify these steps, not only to create opportunities for myself but to also help others in the world who are struggling to figure out what actions they should take to achieve their goals and fulfill their dreams."

As part of this quest, Dr. White has examined

the lives of over eighty highly successful people, looking for common themes and patterns of action, and she has written two books based on her findings. "I don't limit myself to one profession or type of endeavor. I study entrepreneurs, doctors, CEOs, athletes, writers, entertainers, politicians, and many others." What she has discovered is that, despite their varied backgrounds, experiences, and areas of expertise, all of these high achievers have taken a common set of steps or series of actions—every one of which is evident in the stories of the entrepreneurs you've met in the preceding pages.

According to Dr. White, highly successful people are united by their ability to:

1. **Identify their strengths and accept their weaknesses.**

   Instead of bemoaning their weaknesses, they focus on developing what they do best and then pursue areas where those strengths will make a difference. In other words, they work their strengths and find others to do the things that they do badly. Richard Branson, the British founder of the Virgin group of businesses, is dyslexic and barely finished secondary school. Soon after he started his first business, he realized that he was terrible at doing the numbers, so he recruited his best friend, Nik Powell, to manage the money.

2. **Find and follow their passion.**
    Succeeding takes thousands of hours of concentrated effort. If you aren't passionate about what you do, you will never be willing to give the time and effort that is needed. Successful people are always passionate about what they do. For them, what they do is not "work." Instead, it is one of the most fulfilling ways that they can spend their time.

3. **Start with a small thought.**
    Most of the people I studied did not start out with grand plans to build an empire or change the world. They started with small intentions which grew and changed as they succeeded. Sam Walton, who founded Walmart, initially

just wanted to build a successful retail store in a small Arkansas town that provided people in the area with goods that they needed at a reasonable price.

4. **Go the extra mile.**

Despite our talents, we all have effort at our disposal. We can always do more when the situation demands it. This is what successful people do. They put forth the extra effort when it counts. Margaret Thatcher, who became the first and, at this date, the only female prime minister of Great Britain, was renowned for the extensive preparation that she did for her debates in the House of Commons. She could always drown her opponent in a barrage of facts that totally left-footed him.

5. **Make themselves visible.**

We think that if we work hard and do a good job, success will follow. This is not enough. I'm always amazed at all the hidden superstars in this world who work hard and do a great job. I see them everywhere. They check me out at the grocery store, repair my car, or help me over the phone with a customer service problem. Unfortunately, most of these people are taken for granted and not rewarded for their talents because no one notices. Managers and people in power tend to notice people below them only when something goes wrong. People who become successful overcome this by finding ways to be recognized for the good work that they do. To do this, they seize opportunities that give them a chance to show higher-level people who can open doors for them what they can do.

When Jack Welch first came to General Electric, he was just one of many new hires and his boss wasn't particularly impressed with him. When Jack's boss's boss asked him to do a cost and physical property analysis of their new plastic, he seized the opportunity to become visible by doing much more than was asked. He didn't just analyze the cost and physical properties of the plastic. He also compared it to competing plastics in the market. His boss's boss was so impressed that he became his mentor and started him on his journey to becoming CEO of GE.

6. **Get others to help.**

No one succeeds alone. Behind every successful person are a group of people who helped them succeed. It was Paul Allen's idea to start Microsoft because he believed that one day everyone would have a personal computer in their home. He had to convince Bill Gates to leave school and join him. Similarly, Steve Jobs also had help. He didn't build the first Apple computer. Steve Wozniack did. Steve Jobs was the one who put forth the enormous effort needed to sell it and find a market niche, but he could never have done this without Steve Wozniak's electronic brilliance.

7. **Take risks.**

We tend to be creatures of habit because habits provide our lives with predictability and a feeling that we are in control of our lives.

This is one of the major reasons that people cling to their thoughts and don't translate them into actions, because actions always have an element of risk. Successful people are willing to take these risks. This doesn't mean that they take foolish risks which have little chance of success. Rather they take calculated risks—ones which have a reasonable chance of success.

8. **Manage failure.**

Successful people are not afraid of failure. For them, it is just feedback or a problem that must be solved. When failure occurs, they face it, accept it, and then take the best action that is available based on the circumstances. J. K. Rowling was on welfare when she wrote the first Harry Potter book and has stated that she considered herself "the biggest failure I knew," but this didn't stop her. She kept writing. In other cases, successful people do a U-turn when they fail. After Sam Walton discovered that he couldn't renew his lease on his first retail store because it was so successful that his landlord wanted it for his son, he didn't spend time bemoaning his fate. Instead, he packed up and started over in another town.

Of the countless men and women who have exhibited these traits and whose lives stand as a testament to their effectiveness, one of the most famous is Abraham Lincoln, the sixteenth president of the United States. By implementing them, he was able to rise to the highest position in the country and live a wealthy and fulfilled life.

He also changed the course of human history.

Abraham Lincoln knew his strengths and weaknesses. He had to struggle to learn and was self-educated. He became a lawyer and, by most standards, created some level of wealth in that career. He could have stopped there and been considered a "success." Instead, he used the visibility and experience he gained in that position to pursue his true interest: politics.

In March 1832, Lincoln campaigned for the Illinois General Assembly but lost. In 1858, he ran for the US Senate and again lost. He also lost the Republican National Convention's nomination for vice president of the United States in 1856. By this time, it was becoming well known that Lincoln was against slavery—which would become the hallmark of his presidency and legacy. Not letting failure stand in his way, he continued to pursue a political career and express his beliefs. Finally, in 1858, Lincoln was elected to the US Senate.

The offspring of Lincoln's thoughts was the abolishment of slavery. By continually taking action, he monumentally transformed the United States and the life of every person in it from that day forward. Imagine the great loss the country would have suffered if he had let not one, not two, but several defeats and disadvantages prevent him from his goal.

You, too, have that potential. You, too, are capable of transforming your life and the lives of others using the magnificent power you were born with: the power of thought. Thoughts have been characterized as "a dime a dozen." People offer "a penny for your thoughts." The irony of these clichés is that our thoughts have value far beyond measure—*if* we take action to make them become reality. The greatest riches you will ever acquire will come to you via your thoughts, the actions you take on them, and the results those actions produce.

The achievement strategies and techniques penned by Napoleon Hill in *Think and Grow Rich* have been absorbed and applied by all of the entrepreneurs in this book. Their successes are the offspring of both his thoughts and actions and their own, as are the successes of those that they, in turn, have inspired . . . and on and on it goes. The ripple effect of *Think and Grow Rich* has been growing for a century, proving that what starts in our minds has the potential to influence and transform lives for all time.

The impact you can make on the world will be as big or small as the thoughts you are thinking. So think *spectacularly* . . . act *now* . . . write your own success story—and keep that ripple going.

ACKNOWLEDGMENTS

Special appreciation goes out to my personal Master Mind group, which participated along this journey.

You are truly one in a million.

Thanks for all you do to make this world a brighter place.

Allyn Reid, Amelia Cai, Angie Fong, Ben Eisenburg, Dave Michael, Diane Bacchus-Quddus, Fabian Tan, Farzan Rajput, Hilliard Goldwyn, Jill Voss, Joan Magill, John Rodgers, Lori Taylor, Lynn Barnes, Matt Wolcott, Michael Drew, Nahaz Quddus, Richard Barrier, and Sandi Shanner.

—GREG S. REID

ABOUT THE AUTHORS

—◆—

To millions of people across the globe, the name **Bob Proctor** is synonymous with success. Long before his role in the movie *The Secret* sent him into the realm of superstardom, he was already a legendary figure in the world of personal development. His insights, inspiration, ideas, systems, and strategies are the dimes on which countless lives have spun— the sparks that have ignited career transformations, personal epiphanies, inner awakenings, and the creation of million-dollar fortunes the world over.

Bob is the heir to the legacy of the modern science of success that began with the financier and philanthropist Andrew Carnegie. Carnegie's great challenge to the young reporter Napoleon Hill to discern a formula for success fueled Hill's creation of the renowned book *Think and Grow Rich*. Upon discovering this book at the age of twenty-six, Bob's life changed in an instant, leading him on his own quest for the secrets of success. That quest led him to Earl Nightingale, the famed "Dean of Personal Development," and his business partner, Lloyd Conant, who soon became Bob's colleagues and mentors. Today, Bob continues to build upon and spread the remarkable teachings of these giants.

As a speaker, author, consultant, coach, and mentor, Bob Proctor works with business entities and individuals around the world, instilling within them not only the mental foundations of success and the motivation to achieve, but also the actionable strategies that will empower them to grow, improve, and thrive in today's ever-changing world. Through the Proctor Gallagher Institute, Bob, alongside cofounder, company president, and CEO Sandra Gallagher, and their team, teach the principles, strategies, and fundamentals that help people and organizations create the results they want in life . . . results that *stick*.

Greg S. Reid—best-selling author, acclaimed speaker, filmmaker, and master storyteller—is a natural entrepreneur known for his giving spirit and for having a knack for translating complicated situations into simple, digestible concepts.

As an action-taking phenomenon, strategy turns into results fast and furious, and relationships are deep and rich in the space he orbits.

www.BookGreg.com

Published in more than forty-five books, twenty-eight best sellers, five motion pictures, and featured in countless magazines, Greg shares that the most valuable lessons we learn are also the easiest ones to apply.

Recently, Greg was hand selected by the Napoleon Hill Foundation to help carry on the teaching found in the bible of personal achievement, *Think and Grow Rich*.

His latest movie, *Wish Man*, features the real-life story of Frank Shankwitz (co-founder of the Make-A-Wish Foundation*), where one boy's desire inspired a man to change the world.

*Featured in *Stickability, The Power of Perseverance*

If you enjoyed this book, visit

www.tarcherbooks.com

and sign up for Tarcher's e-newsletter to receive
special offers, giveaway promotions, and
information on hot upcoming releases.

TARCHER
PENGUIN

Great Lives Begin with Great Ideas

Connect with the Tarcher Community

• • •

Stay in touch with favorite authors!
Enter weekly contests!
Read exclusive excerpts!
Voice your opinions!

Follow us

 Tarcher Books

 @TarcherBooks

If you would like to place a bulk order
of this book, call 1-800-847-5515.